Memories
of
Colchester

Part of the
Memories
series

*The Publishers would like to thank the following companies for supporting
the production of this book*

Main Sponsor

Hatfields Furnishers Limited

CA Blackwell (Contracts) Limited

RG Carter Colchester

Cullum

Essex Heating Supplies Limited

TJ Evers Limited

CH Lindsey & Son Limited

MG Electric (Colchester) Limited

Osborne Garages

The Prior Associated Companies

Rose of Colchester Limited

First published in Great Britain by True North Books Limited
Units 3 - 5 Heathfield Industrial Park
Elland West Yorkshire
HX5 9AE
Tel. 01422 377977
© Copyright: True North Books Limited 1999

ISBN 1 900463 74 1

Text, design and origination by True North Books Limited
Printed and bound by The Amadeus Press Limited

Introduction from Hatfields of Colchester

John Hatfield, founder
1847-1930

John R London, Chairman
1920-1983

We do hope that you enjoy reading this special edition of the Memories of Colchester. Hatfields was both flattered and delighted to have been invited to be the sponsors of this book.

Colchester is the oldest recorded town in England with a wonderful history. We feel uniquely privileged as a family business, now well over a hundred years old, to have borne witness to so many of the changes that have taken place in the last century.

Our continued success as the oldest and largest Furnishing Store in Colchester is due to many reasons. However, number one has to be our Staff. Our policy has always been to provide friendly, courteous, efficient and honest service. These are fine words, but without a dedicated and caring staff they would be just that. We are proud to say we have such staff.

We have upheld the examples of the two men - to whom we would like to dedicate this book. Without them, there would be no Hatfields today.

H Tony London
Hatfields of Colchester

Established over 100 years and still a family business

Voted by the furniture trade the best independent furniture store in the country

Contents

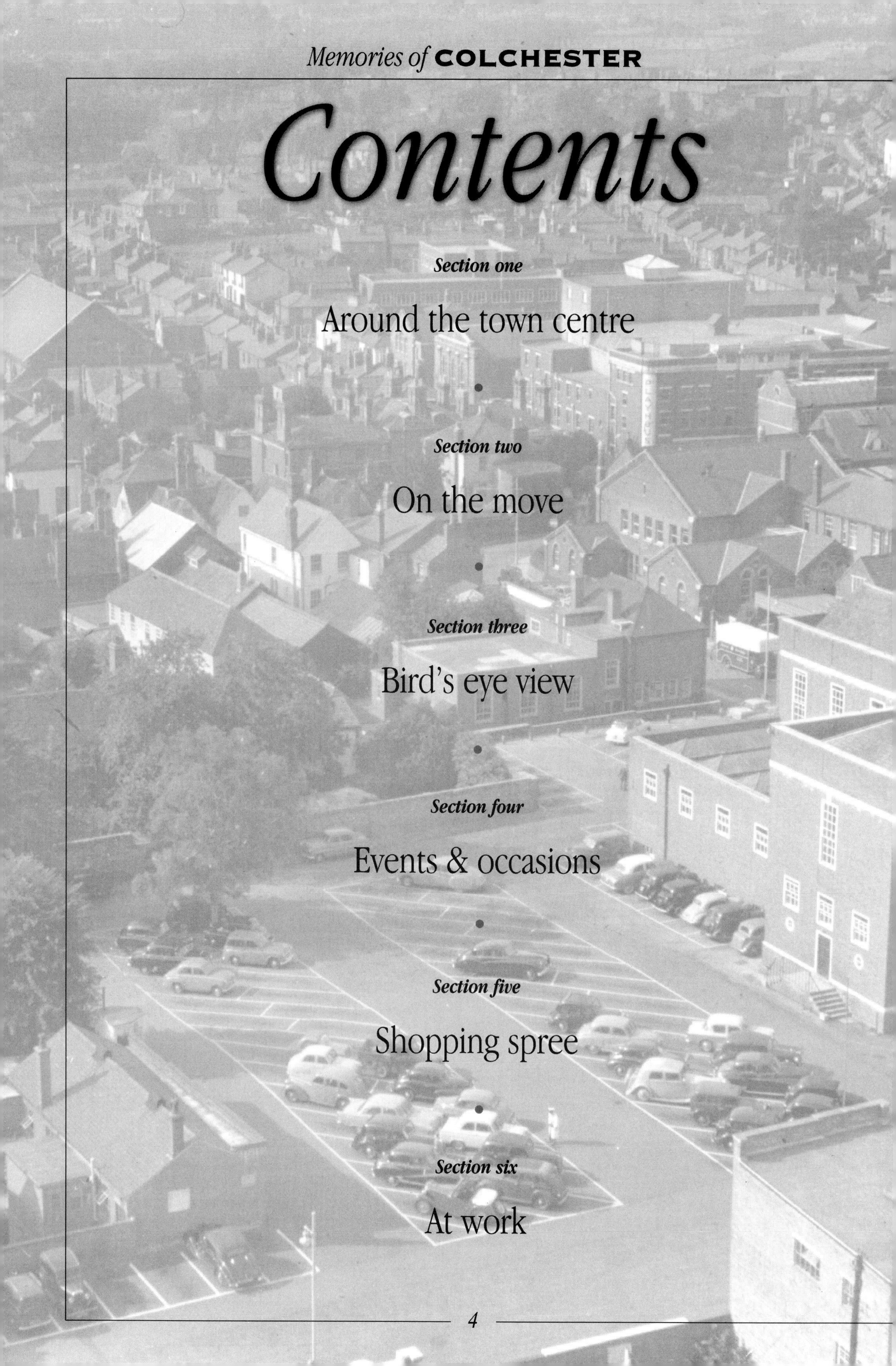

Section one

Around the town centre

•

Section two

On the move

•

Section three

Bird's eye view

•

Section four

Events & occasions

•

Section five

Shopping spree

•

Section six

At work

Around the town centre

The times they are a-changing. In 1925, there was as great a variety of traffic on Head Street as ever could have been seen. The motor car was driving along next to the bicycle. Along the road, the trams rattled and the horses still pulled LNER wagons bound for the railway goods yard. A whole stream of cars was heading down the hill from High Street corner. Opposite the Co-op building, the name 'Hat and Frock Showroom' has a lovely period ring to it. Some towns started to suffer traffic congestion after the second world war. Our town was decades ahead of its time, by the look of this street

scene. To the right is the start of St Isaac's Walk. Sir Isaac Rebow was the town's MP, as were the next two generations of his family. As simple Isaac Rebow, he entertained King William III in his home, which stood on the northwest corner of the Walk. The monarch must have been impressed, because Isaac was knighted in 1693. Not only is the Rebow family remembered here, there is also Rebow Street, off King Stephen Road. This was named in memory of Sir Isaac's father, John (1628-99). King William's host followed his father to the grave in 1726.

Events of the 1930s

HOT OFF THE PRESS
The years of the 1930s saw Adolf Hitler's sickening anti-Jewish campaign echoed in the streets of Britain. On 19th October 1936 Oswald Mosley's 7,000-strong British Union of Fascists clashed head on with thousands of Jews and Communists in London, resulting in 80 people being injured in the ensuing battle. Mosley and his 'blackshirts' later rampaged through the streets beating up Jews and smashing the windows of their businesses.

GETTING AROUND
At the beginning of the decade many believed that the airship was the transport of the future. The R101 airship, however, loaded with thousands of cubic metres of hydrogen, crashed in France on its maiden flight in 1930. Forty-eight passengers and crew lost their lives. In 1937 the Hindenburg burst into flames - the entire disaster caught on camera and described by a distraught reporter. The days of the airship were numbered.

SPORTING CHANCE
In 1939 British racing driver Sir Malcolm Campbell hit the headlines when he captured the world's water-speed record for the third time in 'Bluebird' - all his cars were given the same name. A racing driver who set world speed records both on land and on water, Sir Malcolm established world land-speed records no fewer than nine times. His son Donald went on to set further records, tragically dying in 1967 when his speedboat - also named 'Bluebird' - crashed.

May 1947 was the start of one of the finest summers within living memory. Temperatures soared and we sweltered in the sun. Cricketers took full advantage of the glorious days. The Middlesex 'twins', Bill Edrich and Denis Compton, went berserk at the crease. They each thrashed the opposition bowling for over 3,000 runs. No pair ever matched that before or since. We needed something to cheer us. The winter had been one of the worst on record. Frozen

Britain worked by candlelight as fuel shortages and power cuts bit hard. We might have won the war, but winning the peace was harder still. The meat ration was reduced to one shilling (5p) a week, pleasure motoring stopped and foreign holidays were banned. We had to rely on the Americans to help us out with financial assistance via the Marshall aid plan. Because of all this, the National Benzole petrol pump near the pillar box should not have had much use. Looking east along Crouch Street, some motorists seem to have been able to manage. Let us hope they were not using the black market that, sadly, grew up out of the crisis. The properties along the north side of Crouch Street changed very little 100 years.

In 1933, looking west along High Street, the banner proudly advertises the town's Rose Show. As with other British towns, there were always special weeks and festivals to be celebrated. Nottingham had its Goose Fair and Harrogate its Yorkshire Show. Colchester was not to be left out. The Oyster Feast, held in October, dated back to medieval times. But, since the 18th century, the town has enjoyed a 'growing' reputation. Colchester roses are known nationwide. The biggest supply comes from the company that Frank Cant established over 230 years ago. Particularly suited to the Essex soil and climate, no other flower is so universally known and admired as the rose. Mention the name 'Harry Wheatcroft' and everyone recognises a famous rose grower. The blossoms range in colour from white through various

Events of the 1930s

SCIENCE AND DISCOVERY

By observing the heavens, astronomers had long believed that there in the constellation of Gemini lay a new planet, so far undiscovered. They began to search for the elusive planet, and a special astronomical camera was built for the purpose. The planet Pluto was discovered by amateur astronomer Clyde Tombaugh in 1930, less than a year later.

WHAT'S ON?

In this heyday of the cinema, horrified audiences were left gasping at the sight of Fay Wray in the clutches of the giant ape in the film 'King Kong', released in 1933. Very different but just as gripping was the gutsy 1939 American Civil War romance 'Gone with the Wind'. Gable's parting words, 'Frankly, my dear, I don't give a damn' went down in history.

ROYAL WATCH

The talking point of the early 1930s was the affair of the Prince of Wales, who later became King Edward VIII, and American divorcee Wallis Simpson. Faced with a choice, Edward gave up his throne for 'the woman I love' and spent the remainder of his life in exile. Many supported him, though they might not have been as keen to do so if they had been aware of his Nazi sympathies, kept strictly under wraps at the time.

tones of yellow and pink to dark crimson and maroon. Many varieties have been bred with beautiful blends of colour. They have attracted famous people to allow their names to be associated with new strains. A cynic might say that the best way to grow them is to put on a white panama, take a trowel in one hand and a gin and tonic in the other; then pass the spade to the wife to do the digging. Despite that, he will be bringing her a dozen of the finest on Valentine's Day.

Right: The period style of the building and the dress of the woman by the steps suggest that this is a scene from the end of the 19th century. The school-children look much more modern, so it must be 50 years later. The biggest clue comes from the edge of the Esso 5-star sign, peeking out by the far gable end. The sign of happy motoring brings us firmly into the middle of the 20th century. This is the old Rose and Crown at 51 East Street. As a pub, it dates back to the 17th century. The name symbolised the end of the Wars of the Roses, over 100 years earlier, when a house was built on this spot. Additions and alterations continued to be made over the intervening years. As a popular drinking house, close to the Ipswich road, it remained busy until Victorian times. Gradually, the coming of the railway took away passing trade and it failed to have its licence renewed in 1913. By 1937, the building was condemned as unfit for habitation, but it was bought by Mrs Faithfull Roper and restored. In 1962, George Hudson regained the licence and the Rose and Crown returned to trade once more.

Below: The roadsweeper is standing on the path of the Roman wall that ran across Queen Street. Its line was from the angle at the side of Wright's building materials shop, straight over the street. Priory Street joins Queen Street at the café on the left. Straight in front of us, St Botolph's Street leads off towards Plough corner. A large modern roundabout on the A134 occupies that site today. Part of High Street was once known as King Street and Queen Street was so named as a balancing act. It had been known as Southgate, as it led towards that particular gate in the town wall. For many centuries, Queen Street was home to the St Denis fair. It marked the opening of the oyster fishery, an important event in the life of the town. The fair began in the Berryfield, east of Queen Street. Here livestock, especially horses, were sold. Part of the activity overflowed onto Queen Street. The chap in the picture would have enjoyed those days. With his brush, he could have made a killing by sweeping up the horse droppings. Keen gardeners have always been anxious to put horse manure on their roses. Remember following the horse and cart round the streets, armed with a bucket and shovel?

Above: The white bands on the telegraph poles and lampposts were not decorations or town logos. They were an essential part of the blackout in the war. Cars used lights that shone through narrow slits in their headlamp covers. All street lamps were switched off and moving along darkened roads was a dangerous manoeuvre. The white markings helped drivers to find their way without too many bumps. St Botolph's school stood on the right of Priory Street. The ruined priory is further off to the right. The buildings on the left have now gone and a large open car park marks the spot. Outside the engineers' yard, the three little maids from school, reminding us of that favourite from the Mikado, seem to have caught the fancy of a future Romeo. Like all girls then and now, they ignore his glances. Perhaps they will have a giggle about him further down the

street. In the distance, two other girls walk along together, while another pair rides up the road. What is it about the fairer sex that they can never go anywhere or do anything, except in company? They even need the toilet in tandem! This was a safer time for them, however. There may have been a war on, but no parents met them from school. There were few worries about strangers in 1940.

Top: It was in the early 1980s that plans were mooted for the redevelopment of Culver Street. These did not come into full fruition until the late 1980s and early 1990s. The whole street scene would change forever. In the main, it is now part of the pedestrianised shopping epicentre of Colchester. Home to the Culver Square and Lion Walk shopping centres, little businesses like Stemp's and Pringle's, that traded here in the 1940s, have disappeared without trace. Standing outside the Royal London Insurance Office, the cloth capped cyclist is looking along Culver Street towards Woolworth's. The larger businesses could survive the changes. Some relocated, some remodelled and stayed put. The one man enterprises generally did not have the reserves or the capital to be able to hang on. They went to the wall. Such is progress. FW Woolworth, the original five and ten cent store, had been building its empire in America since 1879. In 1911 the company arrived in Liverpool and quickly expanded its influence across the country. By 1940, there were few major British towns that did not boast a 'Woolie's'. The smartly dressed couple crossing Culver Street probably did their shopping in more upmarket outlets. The Woolworth store was more likely to attract cloth caps than Oxford bags.

Events of the 1930s

MELODY MAKERS

Throughout the 1930s a young American trombonist called Glenn Miller was making his mark in the world of music. By 1939 the Glenn Miller sound was a clear leader in the field; his clean-cut, meticulously executed arrangements of numbers such as 'A String of Pearls' and 'Moonlight Serenade' brought him fame across the world as a big-band leader. During a flight to England from Paris in 1944 Miller's plane disappeared; no wreckage was ever found.

THE WORLD AT LARGE

In India, Gandhi's peaceful protests against British rule were gathering momentum. The Salt Laws were a great bone of contention: forced to buy salt from the British government, thousands of protestors marched to the salt works, intending to take it over in the name of the Indian people. Policemen and guards attacked the marchers, but not one of them fought back. Gandhi, who earned for himself the name 'Mahatma' - Great Soul - was assassinated in 1948.

INVENTION AND TECHNOLOGY

With no driving tests or speed restrictions, 120,000 people were killed on the roads in Britain between the two world wars. In 1934 Percy Shaw, invented a safety device destined to become familiar the world over: reflecting roadstuds. In dark or foggy conditions the studs that reflected light from the car's headlights kept traffic on the 'straight and narrow' and must over the years have saved many lives.

Moving up Head Street from the Norwich Union office and FC Winch's wine merchant shop, the camera has panned up the northern end towards North Hill. Opposite the junction with High Street, the original post office holds centre stage. It had done so since 1874. The more modern looking southern extension dates from the 1930s and had only been open for a few years when this picture was taken. Beyond the post office, the Army and Navy stores did good business

in trading strong and sturdy clothing and footwear. The store had once been a pub, the Alexandra Inn. It owed its name to Princess Alexandra, daughter of Christian IX of Denmark. She married the future British king, Edward VII, in 1863. Alexandra died at Sandringham in 1925. It was lucky that the building was not given her full name or it would have been the Alexandra Caroline Mary Charlotte Louisa Julia, Princess of Schleswig-Holstein-Sonderburg-Glacksburg. A sign writer would have loved that. The pub was supposed to be haunted by the ghost of the landlord's daughter who was murdered by a Chelmsford railway worker. So seriously was this taken that the building was exorcised in the 1950s, 40 years since it ceased to be an inn.

North Hill leads towards Middlesborough and the River Colne. The Marquis of Granby pub sold Truman's ales across the road from the Avery scale and weighing machine makers. The motor cyclist riding north is crossing the line of the Roman wall. He is passing the spot where the arch of the north gate once stood. The Market Tavern, also known as the New Cattle Market Inn, to the left of the motorbike, was a popular watering hole for thirsty farmers. They had come to trade at the livestock and farm produce market that flourished next door to the tavern. The market had moved to Middlesborough from High Street in 1862. It stayed there for a century, before being relocated to Severalls Lane in the 1970s. Whether the tavern would have survived the loss of the custom of those lusty sons of the soil was never tested. In 1974, it had to go to make way for the construction of the

Events of the 1940s

WHAT'S ON?
In wartime Britain few families were without a wireless set. It was the most popular form of entertainment, and programmes such as ITMA, Music While You Work and Workers' Playtime provided the people with an escape from the harsh realities of bombing raids and ration books. In 1946 the BBC introduced the Light Programme, the Home Service and the Third Programme, which gave audiences a wider choice of listening.

GETTING AROUND
October 1948 saw the production of Britain's first new car designs since before the war. The Morris Minor was destined for fame as one of the most popular family cars, while the four-wheel-drive Land Rover answered the need for a British-made off-road vehicle. The country was deeply in the red, however, because of overseas debts incurred during the war. The post-war export drive that followed meant that British drivers had a long wait for their own new car.

SPORTING CHANCE
American World Heavyweight Boxing Champion Joe Louis, who first took the title back in 1937, ruled the world of boxing during the 1930s and 40s, making a name for himself as unbeatable. Time after time he successfully defended his title against all comers, finally retiring in 1948 after fighting an amazing 25 title bouts throughout his boxing career. Louis died in 1981 at the age of 67.

western relief road. There was a public outcry and campaign against the loss of yet another piece of history. The council listened, consulted, considered and then acted as all councils do. It carried on regardless and the tavern was no more. It was later discovered, during the time of the road excavations, that the tavern had once been the site of a 15th century building and could also trace the remains of Roman villa that were found back to the 3rd century. The Royal London Insurance Company has its offices there these days.

Bottom: St John's Street was named after the abbey that was founded in 1096 on the road to Mersea. The 17th century building that stands behind the lamppost has given way to Century House. In 1940 such developments were some way off. It looks like a quiet day in a peaceful town that could have been lifted from any era. The pair on the right, near the entrance to the 1936 bus park, provide the clue to the reason for the gentleness of the day. It is wartime. The streets are quiet because times are hard and cars can only be used sparingly. These soldiers are on leave. For them it is but a brief moment in time when they can pretend that things are normal. Perhaps they were part of the summertime shambles that was Dunkirk. Operation Dynamo had turned disaster into a rescue that saved many of our brave lads. Over 300,000 were brought back from the beaches, but many thousands more never made it. For one hero it was a chance to be a dad again. He could take his son into town and remember what it was like to walk hand in hand with him under a free sky. Soon, it would be time to return to his regiment. He might never have a chance to be a father again.

Right: A number of the town shops have fake Tudor fronts. There is one on Crouch Street, just round the corner from Headgate. It has had many changes of use over the years. At the beginning of the 21st century it housed a takeaway pizzeria, which seemed out of keeping with the facade. Further along there is a mixture of minicab offices,

pubs and a cinema. In 1940 it had some smarter shops. William Smith was a 'progressive florist and fruiterer'. It is hard to understand what he meant, but it sounded modern and forward thinking. The shoe shop on the corner had the same idea. There was a new look to be had, but with the same old care being taken. The old chap gazing at the window from across the road does not look too impressed. Perhaps the cost of soling and heeling shoes is puzzling him. Ladies' shoe repair was done for half a crown, but men's was charged at 3s 9d. That was a 50 per cent price difference. Were men's feet half as big again? Their egos might have been, but surely not their 'plates of meat'. To anyone under about 35, those prices meant 12.5p and 19p. You can't get a shoelace for that.

Above: Head Street led to the head or chief gate on the town walls. To add a little flavour to the name of the street, the severed heads of rebels were placed there as a warning to the rest of the population. This gory practice continued into the days of the civil war. There is a record of a head being impaled there as late as 1756. The cyclists have just passed Church Walk, alongside the CIS building. Beyond the shops of Berner, Ranson and Luckin-Smith, the imposing building housed the gas showroom. Business continued there until the late 1990s, when it was closed. The Norwich Union office completes this set of premises. Co-operative Insurance was one of the spin-off businesses from the little pioneer enterprise of a grocery shop in the middle of the 19th century. Cycling was both a pleasant pastime and a necessary form of travel at the start of the 1940s as cars and petrol were in short supply. Those bikes were fairly heavy and three Sturmey-Archer gears were the best you could hope for to help cope with some of the more hilly stretches. The modern pushbike, with its drop handlebars and 21 geared drive wheel, is a doddle in comparison.

Right: Culver Street is in the heart of Colchester that has seen the greatest building and development changes of recent years. Now divided into east and west sections, separated by the Lion Walk shopping centre, it is largely pedestrianised. In 1940 you could walk its complete length. In the distance, the building with the sloping roof used to contain a gymnasium. The Bunting Rooms sounded to the grunts and puffs of healthy exercise. It was not called pumping iron then, but the routines were the same, even if the equipment was less sophisticated. The van is parked outside the Lay and Wheeler wine vaults. These huge receptacles stretched underground across to High Street. Colchester had its very own wine lake, in those days. Bentham Printing Works produced a variety of publications, but its main function was to publish the Essex County Standard. News of the war dominated the headlines, but there were some other stories around that gave a little light relief from the sombre stories coming from Europe. Our own Vivien Leigh and Robert Donat had won Oscars for their parts in 'Gone with the Wind' and 'Goodbye Mr Chips'. Bogskar had won the Grand National. We could celebrate our winnings with a dip in that wine lake.

A visit to the barber was a man's thing. Women went to the hairdresser. Unisex was unheard of. To a Colcestrian, 60 years ago, it might have been something dubious on a one wheeled bicycle. In Webb's you could get a hot towel to finish off a really close shave from a cut-throat razor. The barber honed the blade on a leather strop and you put your trust in his accuracy. The haircut was straightforward. A good short back and sides would see you right for weeks to come. A touch of brilliantine on top and a 'little something for the weekend' rounded off the visit. Pelham's Lane is a little cut through from Culver Street to High Street.

All these buildings, pictured in 1942, have disappeared or been drastically altered. A little health food shop and jeweller's, plus a few other shops, are there now. Looking north, there was once a Norman stone house on the far corner. It was destroyed in the 18th century. Four hundred years before that, it was home to a wealthy man known as Master John, after whom the lane was once called. Later it was named Whitefotes Lane. Robert Whitfott was a rich merchant and his memory lived on in the lane. The last person to have the honour was shopkeeper William Pelham. He became a councillor in 1623 and served for 20 years.

into ruin. A new design by Sir Gilbert Scott saw St Nicholas Church rise again in 1876. Its beautifully crafted spire was an attractive sight for nearly 80 years. Regrettably, by the time of this photograph, the grim reaper was getting ready to make his move. The last services were held in 1952 and the building was demolished in 1955, though the churchyard survived as a garden behind St Nicholas House.

Top: There may be a war on, but there is still work to be done. People are crossing Culver Street from one side of Long Wyre Street to the other. A culvert or drain would seem to be the obvious source of the name of Culver Street.

Above: By the time the late 1940s had arrived, the attractive St Nicholas Church had only a few years to go. Seen from the western end of High Street, the church was a victim of many Anglican churches that could be found in and around the town. Congregations, although larger than those of today, had shrunk from the numbers that could be expected in the first half of the 20th century. Perhaps some people had left their faith behind on the killing fields of Europe or the evil prison camps in Japan. Whatever the reason, income fell from smaller contributions on the collection plates. Repairs, needed because of the passage of time or the ravages of war, were too costly for some to bear. There was a church on this site as long ago as the 12th century. Two centuries later it was replaced by a small one with a central tower, but in the 18th it had fallen

Sometimes things are not so straightforward. Culver is an old English word that means dove or pigeon. There was once a dovecote nearby, just to the east of Queen Street. In earlier times, this was Back Lane. The reason for that name is the one you would expect from the street's location. Jack's, with its cigarette adverts, is a good place for a bargain. As a form of army surplus store it has long been the place to get a good deal. Locals price up an item in the more upmarket shops and then come down here to get the equivalent at half the price. Canny may be a northeast word, but the inhabitants of Colchester know the meaning well. The railings of St Nicholas Church are now the place where the homeless and helpless gather in the evening. A soup kitchen is set up and the less fortunate can get a hot meal.

Events of the 1940s

HOT OFF THE PRESS

At the end of World War II in 1945 the Allies had their first sight of the unspeakable horrors of the Nazi extermination camps they had only heard of until then. In January, 4,000 emaciated prisoners more dead than alive were liberated by the Russians from Auschwitz in Poland, where three million people, most of them Jews, were murdered. The following year 23 prominent Nazis faced justice at Nuremberg; 12 of them were sentenced to death for crimes against humanity.

THE WORLD AT LARGE

The desert area of Alamogordo in New Mexico was the scene of the first atomic bomb detonation on July 16, 1945. With an explosive power equal to more than 15,000 tons of TNT, the flash could be seen 180 miles away. President Truman judged that the bomb could secure victory over Japan with far less loss of US lives than a conventional invasion, and on 6th August the first of the new weapons was dropped on Hiroshima. Around 80,000 people died.

ROYAL WATCH

By the end of World War II, the 19-year-old Princess Elizabeth and her distant cousin Lieutenant Philip Mountbatten RN were already in love. The King and Queen approved of Elizabeth's choice of husband, though they realised that she was rather young and had not mixed with many other young men. The engagement announcement was postponed until the Princess had spent four months on tour in Africa. The couple's wedding on 20th November 1947 was a glittering occasion - the first royal pageantry since before the war.

Looking west along High Street, Colchester appears to be a town of women and old men. The young men have volunteered or been conscripted to go off and fight for the freedom of their families. The women ride their bicycles, filling the panniers with whatever is available to make a meal for those left behind. They had taken the lead in keeping the home fires burning in the first world war. This new battle with Germany and the Axis powers would bring out the

best in them, yet again. There would be ambulances to drive, factories to be worked and land to be tilled. Many women would combine these jobs with the task of bringing up children and keeping the home going. The wartime slogan 'be like dad, keep mum' urged people to guard against careless talk. It was not really based on fact. Dad was not there. It was mum who was keeping body and soul together. The woman riding towards the camera past Weddel's chemist shop has plenty to think about. She has to eke out the food and clothing ration to see her family through the week. Having made plans for that, she could be off to the WVS centre to sort through salvaged material for the war effort or down to a factory sorting machine parts for a tank engine.

Above: The little girl on the corner need not worry about the traffic flow. She can cross safely; there is little about. The trams ran along here from 1904 onwards, but they had been gone for over 10 years. It is a different story today as cars pour down from High Street and up from East Hill. Meeting at this point, they all turn down Queen Street as part of the one way system. The shop on the corner is now the Visitors' Information Centre. All Saints Church, with its rectory further along, is now a natural history museum. Once, there was a Norman church on the site. It was built directly opposite to the castle. Only the south wall of the church nave is left. Henry Hayward restored its 14th century tower in the late 1850s. During the war, even trees were not safe from the painted stripes that marked the line of the road or warned of large obstructions. During the blackout many drivers were glad to be able to pick out the white bands and save their bumpers and wings from damage. Peering through the darkness, the markings acted like little lighthouses. The girl on the kerb might just be a 1940s Grace Darling, ready to row to the rescue.

Above right: The photographer has picked a good place from which to point his camera. Perched precariously on the roof of the Essex and Suffolk Fire Office, he could, at least, have organised an insurance policy on his life in case he overbalanced. In July 1935, at the west end of High Street, next to Stead and Simpson, Scott's (Toni's) has just been demolished. It was to be the site of the Palleate Restaurant in coming days. Further development meant that it was turned into the Post Office. High Street was part of the main Roman road and it once ran straight across the demolition site to Balkerne Gate, on the town wall. To get there now, a short detour round to the right is required. The Jumbo, at the top of the picture, is affectionately nicknamed after an elephant that was part of the Barnum and Bailey circus. Victorians were not renowned for a sense of humour, but this water tower must have tickled them. Built in 1882 by Charles Cross, it never squirted water out of its trunk like its namesake, but its solid size and shape has meant that the name stuck.

Right: The bike and sidecar is not often seen on our roads today. In the first half of the 20th century they were much more common. Sometimes they were used to carry a load, but more often there was a passenger on board. The better ones had a cover and hood to keep out the British weather. Even so, they were draughty and chilly to sit in. They were not the safest of vehicles, being vulnerable in a crash. The rider has just come past Cullingford's stationery and marquee hire shop and the Albert Hall art gallery on High Street. The Co-op bank has its home here now. The motor cyclist felt that his cloth cap would protect him just as well as any crash helmet. His attitude would not have gone down well in the Essex and Suffolk Fire Office behind him. That fine building, with its Doric pillars, was the centre for people who insured against risks. His safety would not have been a good bet. The Essex and Suffolk was established in 1802 and held its first meetings in the house of Mrs Slythe, on High Street. Next year it took over part of the Exchange, site of the old corn market. At first it was heavily involved in fire insurance of farms and equipment. Outbreaks of arson in the countryside damaged business and encouraged the company to support the establishment of Colchester Fire Brigade. It maintained various brigades in rural areas until 1902.

Appropriately, the building was constructed from cast iron and stone, both fire resistant materials.

Below: Looking up East Hill towards High Street, the brewer's dray is parked just past the opening to Priory Street. In the distance, the corner of the Minories can just be glimpsed. Victorians coined its name as it sounded quite posh. Built in 1776, it is an art gallery that was opened under the terms of the Batte-Lay bequest. The top of St James' Church peeks over the top of the Ship public house. St James is the largest of the town's ancient parish churches. Like many churches of the Middle Ages, it was built in a grand style and can trace its history to the 12th century. It underwent restoration in the 17th century and again in 1871. The barrels first rolled into the cellars of the Ship in 1764, though its old timber frame dated from the previous century. Owned variously since 1885 by the Colchester Brewing Company, Ind Coope and Allied Breweries, trade dropped off in the 1970s and it closed in 1980. It was converted to a private dwelling in 1992. This picture, taken during the second world war, reminds that pedal power became an important means of transport. Fortunately, the dray had enough of a petrol ration to keep the Ship's customers happy.

Events of the 1940s

MELODY MAKERS
The songs of radio personalities such as Bing Crosby and Vera Lynn were whistled, sung and hummed everywhere during the 1940s. The 'forces' sweetheart' brought hope to war-torn Britain with 'When the Lights go on Again', while the popular crooner's 'White Christmas' is still played around Christmas time even today. Who can forget songs like 'People Will Say we're in Love', 'Don't Fence Me In', 'Zip-a-dee-doo-dah', and 'Riders in the Sky'?

INVENTION AND TECHNOLOGY
Inspired by quick-drying printers' ink, in 1945 Hungarian journalist Laszlo Biro developed a ballpoint pen which released viscous ink from its own reservoir as the writer moved the pen across the page. An American inventor was working on a similar idea at the same time, but it was Biro's name that stuck. A few years later Baron Bich developed a low cost version of the pen, and the 'Bic' ballpoint went on sale in France in 1953.

SCIENCE AND DISCOVERY
In 1943 Ukrainian-born biochemist Selman Abraham Waksman made a significant discovery. While studying organisms found in soil he discovered an antibiotic (a name Waksman himself coined) which was later found to be the very first effective treatment for tuberculosis. A major killer for thousands of years, even the writings of the ancient Egyptians contain stories of people suffering from tuberculosis. Waksman's development of strep-tomycin brought him the 1952 Nobel Prize for Medicine.

The George Farmer business still plies its trade from this site on the corner of High Street and Museum Street 60 years later. Today, its sign advertises woodwork supplies, but little more has changed. The same cannot be said for the church of St Nicholas. That was demolished in 1955. At one time, different sections of High Street were given over to varying trades and retail outlets. In one section you could find a group of clothing

shops and, in another, several selling groceries. Looking at the scene from Long Wyre Street, with Jack's cheap and cheerful establishment off to the right, the little fish market is in full swing. Buckets of ice and cold, clammy fingers served the shoppers anxious to get some fresh and substantial food into their baskets. In 1940, the German navy's threat to shipping meant the large merchant vessels and little fishing smacks had a rough time putting food on our tables. People had to be quick to get to the market and snap up whatever there was to be had. Ration books were all very well, but there had to be food provided before it could be rationed. You could not eat a coupon.

Above: *A dismal time on High Street as the drizzle makes this day in 1944 one to forget. At the far end of the road, the Jumbo water tower holds pride of place, as it had done for over 60 years. The traffic is still running both ways, as the one way system did not begin to operate until 1963. From that date, visitors to the town began to go round in circles trying to find their way to destinations that seemed impossible to get to. Life was simpler in those earlier days. Every town has its high street, whether or not it calls it such. Not many towns can boast the history that this one has seen. As the oldest recorded town in the country, the borough has been administered from the same plot of land on High Street since 1160. The ground may now hold an official town hall, but burgesses and lawmakers carried out their official business from the same spot over eight centuries before. The 1086 Domesday Book, William the Conqueror's survey of the nation, ranked the town as the fifth in terms of taxation. It was here he built a royal castle, recognising the strategic importance of the area. The connection with things military goes back to the Iron Age, when early Britons had a form of military base here. The Romans built their stronghold in the centre of the modern town and High Street ran the full east-west length of the area formed by the old walls. Colchester became the country's main garrison town in 1794 and it was to be an important transit camp for troops during both world wars. Different races and peoples tramped High Street for thousands of years. On this dirty day in 1944, it was beginning to look as if it was not going to be the Germans' turn to march the streets as a conquering force. For a while it had been touch and go. The news from abroad was good. Allied forces had made a successful landing on the beaches of Normandy and were pushing across France towards the homeland of the little dictator. Paris had been liberated and the British, under Earl Jellicoe, were in Athens. All that was good news to bring a little brightness to the grey skies. Within 12 months High Street would be alive with colour and excitement. The lampposts would be festooned with flags and bunting as VE and VJ Day arrived. The clouds would clear and bluebirds fly above the white cliffs of Dover and Brightlingsea marshes as well.*

The town hall dominates the High Street and much of the Colchester skyline. Its tall clock, the Victoria tower, was built at the personal expense of Alderman James Paxman in the early 20th century. It is topped by a figure of St Helena facing Jerusalem. The tip of the cross she holds is 162 feet from the ground. There are several legends about her existence. Some believe her to be the daughter of old king Cole, of nursery rhyme fame. Born in either AD 242 or AD 248, she was the mother of Constantine the Great, the first Roman emperor to embrace Christianity. Her husband was killed at York, on an expedition to Britain. She is credited with discovering Christ's cross at Golgotha. More certain is the history of the George, on the right. Once a 15th century house, Thomas Jepson took over licensing rights in 1494. By the 18th century it had become a regular stopover for horse drawn wagons travelling between East Anglia and London. The arrival of the railway in 1843 put a stop to that trade. It is said that William Corder spent a night handcuffed to a bed here in 1828, on his way to be hanged in Bury St Edmunds. He was the murderer of Maria Marten and was made more famous by the Victorian melodrama about the evil doings in the red barn.

On the move

Above: Conductor and driver pose proudly in front of the cab of their Colchester Corporation bus. Although the country's first conductresses, or clippies as they were affectionately known, had been seen in service in 1916, there were very few employed in Colchester between the two world wars. Transport was still largely a male preserve. The lessons learned in the Great War, when women undertook many traditional male roles, were not fully learned until world war two. Even then, it would be a long time before women were accepted behind the wheel of public transport vehicles. They could punch tickets, but driving was a different matter. The fact that they ferried the wounded in ambulances, manoeuvred tractors across ploughed fields or thundered along the byways with wagon loads of scrap metal was quickly forgotten. Driving a bus would have been child's play in comparison. The prototype for this bus had an open top deck. 'Plenty of room up top' would not have interested passengers when the rain was lashing down. It was not long before the enclosed coachwork became standard. Even then, the access to the top deck from the footplate was via an open stairway that could get slippery when the heavens opened.

Right: Arms akimbo for one and standing to attention for the other, these two Colchester Corporation employees worked as a team. Ready for the journey to North Station, they had separate jobs to do; but those combined to provide one service. On a bad day they might have had to tie a rope to the starting handle to get the bus going. The driver was marooned in his cab and had to rely on his partner for signals to stop or move off again. The conductor was more than a ticket seller. He communicated the intentions of passengers to his colleague and helped the elderly on and off the bus with a cheery word. The kind ones gave the kids the end of the ticket roll to play with. Those with a mean streak kept the bus at the bus stop as a late passenger ran towards it. Carefully judging the distance between runner and bus and the speed at which he was sprinting, the skilful conductor could judge his 'hold very tight please' and ding-ding of the bell to perfection. The bus would draw away and the breathless runner was left a yard short! There were not many like that. Most were cheerful chaps and provided the inspiration for the ITV sitcom 'On the Buses', popular in the 1970s, when Reg Varney did battle with bus inspector Stephen Lewis.

Above: Opposite FJ Everitt tailor's and the Achille Serre cleaning and dyeing shop, the workman carefully carries out repairs to the surface of High Street. In 1925 there were few cars to be seen. People used their legs to get around, either pedalling their bikes or using Shanks' pony. Have you ever tried to suggest to your children that they go for a walk or get on their bikes these days? They look at you as if you are daft. For the youth of today, legs are made to press accelerator pedals. Ordinary folk could not afford cars, 75 years ago. The alternative to walking was to take the tram. The workman is trying his best to keep that form of public transport running. Kneeling between the lines, he was not one of the breed that works by leaning on a shovel. Hammer in hand, he has come to deal with the large bump that mysteriously appeared in the middle of the road one Saturday lunchtime. It had been a wet summer and the wooden blocks between the tracks had become soft. Water action had forced grit in between the blocks and the damp caused them to swell. The solid grit and tramlines gave no room for expansion and so up popped the bump.

Above right: On its way out of the bus station towards Monkwick, to the south of town, this 56 seater is just about to pass the bus station café. The vehicle is typical of those in use after the second world war. This model did good service, running from 1945 until 1964. This Bristol K6A had a Duple utility body, if the shoppers being taken home really cared. They were happy to have left the draughty old bus shelters behind. Those contraptions might have kept out a downpour that came straight down, but did not do much to protect those waiting from the wind and driving rain. There were days when it could whistle down the lines of shelters with more chilling effect than a mother-in-law's breath. At least you could get on the bus when it arrived and wait in the dry for it to set off again. These days, it pulls into a terminus and what does the driver do? He jumps off and locks the doors behind him. We are left out in the cold while he nips off for a brew. What does he think a row of middle aged housewives is going to do whilst he is away? Have some sort of wild party until he gets back? Fat chance. The shelters were eventually demolished and replaced by a multi storey car park. That has now gone, as well.

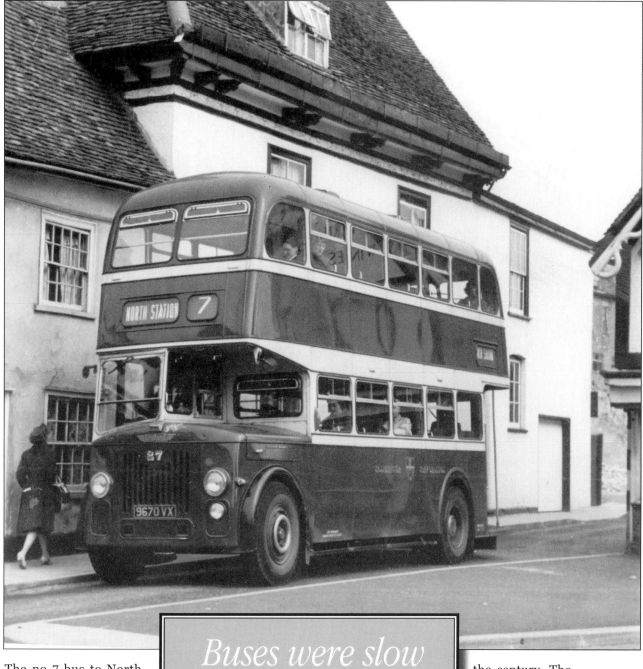

Buses were slow to arrive in the town as it was well served by its tram system

The no 7 bus to North Station is coming from the now pedestrianised Vineyard Street. It has almost reached the Osborne Street/St John's Street junction, as it passes the Brewer's Arms. It has been a pub since 1805 and is true to its name. Beer really was brewed on site. The building is even older. It was erected in 1738, when it was Nutshell Hall. The bus is a Leyland PD2/31, with a Massey body built on a 1960 chassis. Buses were slow to arrive in Colchester, as it had been well served by its trams earlier in the century. The Corporation provided for what it called 'tramway abandonment' in 1927. One year later, the first buses were purchased. These were four Dennis G models that were capable of carrying 20 seated passengers. In 1928, the trams on Eastgates route were replaced with two new bus services. On 1st October of the same year, buses took over the Lexden to North Station journey. The death knell of the tram service was beginning to be rung. The 60s bus in the picture could carry three times as many passengers as the first ones the town saw.

Bird's eye view

Having been given its charter by Richard the Lionheart Colchester began to develop as a market and clothmaking town

Looking north towards the town centre, across Magdalen Street and the link roads to the A134, it is easier to imagine the little settlement that began here hundreds of years before Christ was born. Down at ground level, there is no sense of the effect that the meandering river and hills had upon early Colcestrians. From the skies it is simpler to notice the ease of access to water and the protection offered by the raised ground. We can get some information from records, excavations and artefacts that have been found, but they are not complete. After the Romans, the Saxons left little for us to discover. Not again, until AD 917, is there a mention of Colchester life, when a Danish garrison was expelled. By the time of 1066 and all that, the borough was a place of some importance, with a mint and a court. St Peter's is mentioned in the Domesday Book. Having been given its town charter by Richard the Lionheart, it developed as a market and clothmaking town. The cloth industry struggled to survive, but was rescued by the 16th century Dutch refugees who fled from their Spanish oppressors. Skilled weavers and cloth workers, their products from the Dutch Bay Hall were famous. The Dutch quarter lies to the north of the town hall.

This approach to the town is being made from the south. The pilot in charge of the aerial shot has followed a flight path from the vicinity of Roman Hill on the Mersea road. A wider picture would have shown more of the residential areas of Colchester. By the end of the 20th century, there were some 100,000 inhabitants in the town itself. Nearly another 60,000 live in the outlying reaches, under Colchester's administrative control. The borough covers about 125 square miles, stretching from Dedham Vale and Constable country in the northeast to the boats and wild life of Mersea Island and the Colne estuary in the south. There was a small settlement here nearly 3,000 years ago. By the first century AD, Shakespeare's Cymbeline (Cunobelinus) ruled from his capital, Camulodunum, named after

Events of the 1950s

WHAT'S ON?
Television hit Britain in a big way during the 1950s. Older readers will surely remember 'Double Your Money, Dixon of Dock Green and 'Dragnet' (whose characters' names were changed 'to protect the innocent'). Commercial television was introduced on 22nd September 1955, and Gibbs SR toothpaste were drawn out of the hat to become the first advert to be shown. Many believed adverts to be vulgar, however, and audiences were far less than had been hoped for.

GETTING AROUND
The year 1959 saw the development of the world's first practical air-cushion vehicle - better known to us as the hovercraft. The earliest model was only able to travel at slow speeds over very calm water and was unable to carry more than three passengers. The faster and smoother alternative to the sea ferry quickly caught on, and by the 1970s a 170-ton car-carrying hovercraft service had been introduced across the English Channel.

SPORTING CHANCE
The four-minute mile had remained the record since 1945, and had become regarded as virtually unbreakable. On 6th May 1954, however, Oxford University student Roger Bannister literally ran away with the record, accomplishing the seemingly impossible in three minutes 59.4 seconds. Bannister collapsed at the end of his last amazing lap, even temporarily losing his vision. By the end of the day, however, he had recovered sufficiently to celebrate his achievement in a London night club!

the Celtic war god. The approximate centre for this was near the present Sixth Form College. Because of its position on the river and with easy access to the sea, trade with the continent was established. Unfortunately, that trade included some unwelcome visitors. The Romans invaded in AD 43 and Camulodunum was an obvious place to attack. Despite being torched by Boadicea in AD 60, during her uprising against the new regime, the town recovered and grew in importance.

Since 1979, a visit to Colchester Library takes the reader into Trinity Square. The building is in the heart of the pedestrianised shopping area, south of High Street. Books are prized possessions and hold such memories in their pages; but we must not allow nostalgia to blind us to modern technological developments. There are now audio tapes, videos and CD-ROMs to back up the entertainment and knowledge gained from the printed word. As long as we remember that each supports the other, rather than replacing it, history is safe and development assured. Despite that, you cannot but help having a sneaking preference for curling up in bed with

a good book. Somehow, holding onto a computer disc does not have the same attraction. Colchester's old library was on West Stockwell Street. It was near the town hall and, eventually, became an extension of it. Its first books were lent out in 1894, but the library moved to the site pictured, near Maldon Road, in 1947. The transfer should have been earlier. It was only ever partially completed, as war broke out before it could be finished. Instead, it acted as a food office for the duration. Designed by Marshall Sisson, the library housed the Samuel Harsnett collection of religious texts and early editions.

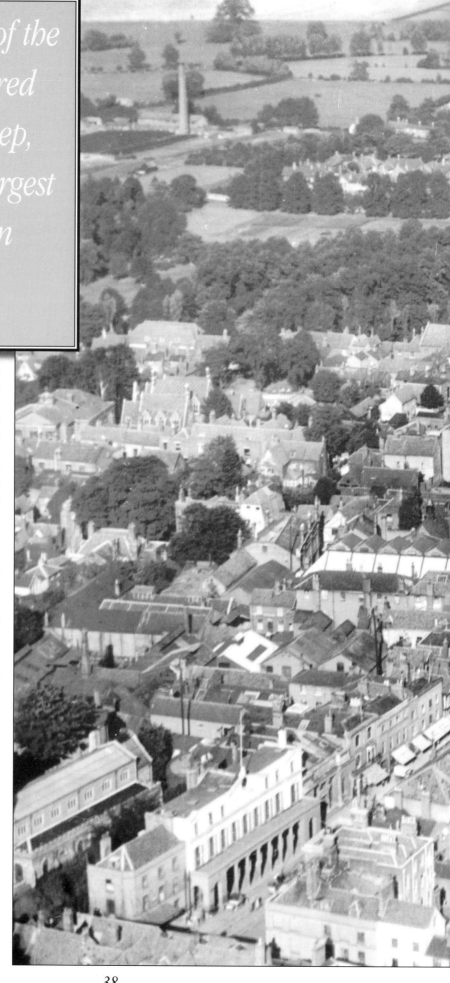

The ramparts of the castle appeared before the keep, which is the largest ever built in Europe

The aerial view of the town shows High Street running diagonally from the bottom left. The trees and lawns of Castle Park make a pretty picture off to the left. The castle itself, is really a castle keep or central building. A great fortress once dominated the area. It stretched from here as far as the north wall of the town. Built by William the Conqueror, the ramparts appeared before the keep arrived, around 1085. They were built over the walls and ruins of the building that had been the temple of Emperor Claudius. He founded Colchester as the first Roman capital of Britain in AD 49. Even so, the keep is the largest that was ever built in Europe. Visitors there today can see one of the finest collections of Roman and British history. It once stood four storeys high. Its chapel reminded many historians of the one in the White Tower of London. The ramparts survive, to the north of High Street. Under them, in 1950, exciting discoveries of the remains of Roman buildings were unearthed. Colchester's famous siege took place in the 17th century, but the castle was the scene of another one, over 400 years before. In 1215, the garrison was forced to surrender to the forces of King John.

Sitting comfortably in Colchester

Over a century ago, in 1886, John Hatfield could be found in his front room at 31 St. John's Street, Colchester dealing in curios. The front room was used to store all his stock during the week's business. Only on Saturday night was it cleared out and gradually restored to its original state so that he and his wife could enjoy the use of a normal front room on Sundays! This enchanting arrangement marked the establishment of Hatfields and the roots of what was to grow into the Colchester family business, known today as Hatfields Furnishers Ltd.

John Hatfield was born in 1847 and before founding Hatfields he worked hard outside the furniture industry. John served as a page boy to the Round family of Birch Hall and later became butler to William Gladstone's son. This work often involved serving the Prime Minister himself on his visits to Hawarden Castle in North Wales. After years of serving others it is no wonder that John's ambition led him to work for himself. His experience in the service industry, however, obviously stood him in good stead when building his own business catering for the needs of his customers.

John Hatfield was a popular character who noted his customers' requirements on his paper shirt cuffs! This primitive paperwork was obviously successful and John's business soon outgrew the front room of his house. To cope with this increase in demand, John acquired buildings across the road from his house and subsequently used them as a warehouse in which to store second-hand furniture. This furniture proved to be popular and indeed was also recently confirmed to be durable. A daughter of a man who purchased some second hand dining chairs from Mr. Hatfield in the 1890s contacted the present day company informing them that the furniture is still in use today, over a hundred years on!

Above left: *John Hatfield, founder of the company.*
Below: *Arthur Hatfield in a picture dating from the late 1910s outside the St John's Street shop.*

John Hatfield and his wife had three sons and three daughters and in 1916 their youngest son, Arthur joined John's business initiating its life as a family firm. The business expanded even further and more premises were purchased. The adjoining properties of 32, 33 and 34 St John's Street were bought for £500. The new site included three cottages, 4, 5 and 6 Sir Isaacs Walk and a yard.

The advent of the first world war brought with it several changes for the Hatfields. Arthur left Colchester to serve his country with the Argyll and Sutherland Highlanders. During this time the greenhouse in the Hatfields new yard proved to be very useful. In a slight diversion from furniture, the grapes growing in the greenhouse were sold over the counter for a halfpenny a pound. When Arthur returned he was faced with the gradual changes affecting the character of St John's Street

including the increasing amount of motor traffic along the road.

The Hatfields resumed business as usual after the war and the firm continued to flourish. However, on the 13th of August 1930 John Hatfield was tragically killed. Minutes after giving his local policeman a photograph of himself, John stepped out in front of an oncoming van and later that afternoon died of his injuries in hospital. The following week a glowing obituary in the Essex Telegraph remembered John Hatfield's interesting and lively character recalling such times as when he appeared in the 1926 Clacton carnival dressed as King Neptune, for which he won a £4 prize!

Five years later Arthur, who had taken over the business since his father's death, decided to sell the St John Street properties. He moved the Hatfield business to 5 Stanwell Street where he continued to trade until 1981.

1943 was an important year for the survival of the Hatfield family business and its future continuation. This was the year that Elsie Hatfield, John Hatfield's daughter, married John London. The link between the Hatfields and the Londons was thus established. After returning from the war, where he had served in the RAF in Iceland and Italy, John London joined his father-in-law in the business. John's younger brother, Tony London, had spent his

Left: Part of the huge purpose-built warehouse.
Above: Arthur Hatfield prior to his retirement with Tony and John at Stanwell Street in 1959.

early working life in the Merchant Navy and the RAF. He subsequently joined his brother in the Hatfield furniture business in 1957.

John and Tony worked for Arthur Hatfield until 1959. By this time Arthur, who had worked for the family business for over four decades, decided to retire and went to live in Hayes Road, Clacton where he stayed until his death, aged 88, in 1975.

John and Tony London purchased the Hatfield furniture business on Arthur's retirement and began to work towards making some changes in order to improve and expand the company. Without any staff John and Tony had to work extremely hard to build up the business. Over the following two years the brothers both worked six days a week and virtually every night, buying, selling and delivering furniture. In between carrying out this work they also managed to fit in some renovation and repair work as well as all the administration. They soon found themselves

needing extra help and just over a year after buying the business they persuaded their elder brother Stanley to join them. Stanley was busy running his own wholesale

confectionery business in North Wales when his brothers asked for his help. He was approaching retirement at this time, and he expected that he would only be needed to work mornings to complete the book-keeping for his brothers and that he would be able to spend his afternoons

leisurely on the golf course. Little did he know what his ambitious brothers had in store with their plans for development.

In 1962 Stanley's son David joined the firm after attending Hawarden grammar school during which

*Above: Peartree Road Store in 1975. The children are Andrew and Robert London. **Top:** A 1970 photograph prior to the opening of the extended St Botolph's showrooms. From left to right: John, Stanley and Tony London in the Ercol showroom. **Left:** Stage and television personality Anita Harris visited the store in April 1980. After the well attended presentation she was presented with a bouquet by Rachel London.*

friendship with Mr Roberts, so much so that it was agreed that they would buy his premises when he retired.

For now though, the London family concentrated on their newest purchase. The old factory buildings at the back of the newly built shop were, for the time being left untouched as warehouse space. The other buildings were converted into showrooms. These showrooms were carpeted throughout, centrally heated and spot-lit and rapidly gained a reputation for being the best furniture showrooms in the town.

The opening day of the new showroom turned out to be a memorable one for everyone concerned, a day that would go down in history. The date was Friday 22nd November and the showroom was opened

time, by a remarkable coincidence, he had taken history lessons in the same castle that John Hatfield had served in many years before. A year later in 1963, the family took the opportunity to bring all their hard work to fruition by expanding the business. In the April of this year a 125 year old confectionery business, C W Hancock in St Botolph's Street, Colchester, came on to the market. The site was purchased by the brothers for £16,500 and Tony was left to organise the conversion of the existing shop, the building work and the opening of the site. The shop adjacent to the new Hatfield shop was a toy shop, Moore and Roberts, owned by Mr Roberts. From the day that the London brothers moved in, they built up a

in the morning without ceremony. An advert had been placed in the local newspapers prior to the event offering a free coffee table with every suite purchased. The Londons were hoping that this would attract a substantial crowd for the first day of trade.

However, two and a quarter hours after opening, not one customer had entered the showroom. This was a disappointment for Hatfields but eventually they managed to sell a fireside chair. The shop

Above left and below: *The 1927 Talbot replica van carries all the cabinet maker's requirement when not in use towing the carnival queen's float.*

stayed open late, until eight at night, but unfortunately the takings for that first day only reached £59.19.6d.

It was only whilst Tony and David were standing outside the showroom, trying to create a crowd effect, that they discovered from a passer-by the reason for such a poor turn out - President John F Kennedy had been assassinated that very day.

Fortunately, the first day's takings were not typical and the new showroom went on to become a success. However, only a year later on the 13th April 1964, the showroom was to suffer another setback. Five fires were started in the town centre, one in the storeroom at the back of the St Botolph's showrooms. The company bounced back from their misfortune and only five months later accidentally stumbled across what was to become a significant promotional technique for Hatfields. A special mink couch was featured in the window of the showroom, on offer at 2,000 guineas. The couch attracted a huge amount of attention and brought large numbers of people in to the shop just to stroke it!

The steadily growing success of the business meant that in the August of 1964 the rest of the St Botolph site could be developed. The storerooms were demolished and replaced with a two floor showroom costing £10,000. The opening of this showroom in 1965 broke records when a £100 advert became the largest ever advert placed in the local paper.

Two years on, in 1967 Hatfields furnished its first showhouse at the prestigious Welshwood Park. The showhouse was soon snapped up for £8,750 and this led to the furnishing of another house on the same estate. This was the first house in the country to be built to metric measurements and therefore secured further publicity for the Hatfields when it was covered by both television networks.

In 1975 the Peartree Road building was acquired. Its office building, car park and warehouse made the site perfect for Hatfields. The ensuing extra work meant that Stanley, far from relaxing on the golf course, took on all legal and financial matters. John supervised the building work and Tony looked after St Botolphs, leaving David to take overall responsibility for the opening of

This page: *Hatfields centenarians lunch.*

Peartree Road. The actual conversion however, did not run smoothly. The construction of the first floor was delayed by a steel strike and at one point the opening deadline seemed beyond their reach. It took eight months to bring the 'empty shell' up to the standard Hatfields demanded. There was a last minute panic though when momentarily, the scissors for the Mayor,

Councillor Joyce Brooks to cut the ribbon with could not be found! These initial hiccups were soon justified when the original sales targets of £600,000 for the first year and £800,000 for the second year were exceeded.

Three years after the opening of Peartree Road, the staff had increased to 44 and a quarter of the first floor was opened as a showroom. This development saw staff from St Botolphs being brought in on Saturdays to meet increasing demands. Eventually, the St Botolph store was

Top: *Hatfields premises today.*
Above: *Hatfield's donated a computer to Philip Morant School in 1985. Pictured are David London with pupil, Claire Slater.* **Right:** *Terry Waite at the company's centenary banquet seen here with the ten local unsung heroes to whom he had presented awards.*

closed. Half of the top floor at the Peartree site was opened to compensate for this closure and additional warehousing was built nearby and opened in 1980.

The old delivery vans were replaced with four Mercedes demountable bodies and two cabs. Also, David's study tour of out-of-town stores in New York and Los Angeles prompted the installation of a new warehouse racking system and fork lift trucks. The business was thriving and maintaining accurate administrative records was increasingly difficult. Hatfields was one of the first family owned retail furnishers in the country to become computerised when, in 1979, a Philips system was installed costing £35,000. This system was upgraded five years later and Hatfields donated the original computer with its six screens to Philip Morant School.

The eighties saw business booming. In 1984 the company appointed a General Manager. Also, a new training office was set up for the staff. It was also in this year that Stanley eventually

retired to catch up with the golf he had been promised over 20 years previously! Television became the main medium for advertising Hatfields. In 1985 the actor Robert Powell starred in a 30 second advert for the company. Unexpectedly, the television advertising even attracted customers from Holland, the Dutch being avid watchers of British TV.

The year 1986 marked 100 years of trading for Hatfields since its establishment in 1886. This auspicious anniversary was celebrated in style by the company who achieved a million pounds in the first sale period of this year. A 1920s style van was added to the fleet and a permanent carnival float was designed, built and donated to the town. A special lunch for local people who had reached their 100th birthday was held and an outing to a theme park was arranged for 100 local children. The company also sponsored a special performance by the London City Ballet at the Mercury Theatre as a tribute to the Hatfield family.

The most spectacular event, however, was the centenary dinner

> *In 1994 the Furniture Trade voted Hatfields the Best Independent Furniture Store in the Country*

held at Colchester Castle to which £5000 was donated for their restoration appeal. A totoal of 100 guests were invited and Terry Waite, the guest of honour, presented awards to ten local unsung heroes! The evening came to a close in grand style when the General Manager, Derek Wyatt, read a letter received from H M The Queen congratulating Hatfields on its centenary.

Left: *The balloon race that Hatfields sponsored was found by Susanna Pyrczek of Luzycka in Poland. Hatfields then arranged for Susanna to visit England as a guest of the company.* ***Top:*** *A trip for 100 children to Pleasure Wood Hills in 1986.*

Hatfields' involvement in the local community continued after the events of the centenary, indeed the company has supported many local causes over the years. One such memorable event took place in 1987 when Hatfields was reported in the local press to have 'brought down the Iron Curtain'. This story stemmed from the St Mary's School balloon race that Hatfields had sponsored. The adventurous winning balloon had managed to travel 700 miles from Colchester all the way to Luzycka in Poland where it was found by Susanna Pyrczek. Hatfields then arranged for Susanna to visit England as a guest of the company for a week where she stayed with Tony London and his family for a holiday of a lifetime!

As the company moved into the nineties it continued to thrive. In 1988 Tony, in association with the manufacturer Sleepeezee, designed a range of divans known as BackChoice, with back sufferers in mind. Following the huge success of this range, Tony was asked to produce a range of beds for the Green Group, the largest furniture buying group in the country. The Green Group had 130 stores, including Libertys of London. A year later a Hatfield range of furniture designed by their chief buyer, Don Massey, and sold in the Colchester store was spotted by a Harrods' furniture buyer who subsequently snapped up the range for the Knightsbridge store. The exceptional success of Hatfields was officially recognised in 1994 when the company was voted the Best

Independent Furniture Store in the country by representatives from the furniture trade.

Today Hatfields boasts the largest furnishing showroom in East Anglia with facilities ranging

from carparks and lifts to baby changing facilities and an in-store coffee shop. The company now employs over 65 staff who are renowned as being 'kind and considerate' and indeed, are helping to ensure that the oldest and largest furniture store in Colchester continues on its steady path of progression for many more years to come.

Above right: Judges from the Furnishing Industry voted Hatfields the Best Independent Retailer in the Country in 1994.
Top: The Hatfields of Colchester Band.
Right: The current board of directors. Front row: David London, Andrew London, Tony London. Standing: Ivan Hawes, Robert Fuller MD.

Events & occasions

Rail disasters are, thankfully, few and far between. For over 150 years we have used trains to take us to work and off on our holidays. The age of steam generated its own nostalgia for generations of youngsters who never grew up. They collected engine numbers and helped preserve old locos and lines that had been consigned to the scrapheap by the likes of the 1960s rail butcher, Dr Beeching. So, when tragedy came, it seemed more of a personal heartache than any plane crash or road accident. In recent years there have been the horrors of Paddington, Clapham and King Cross. In the 1970s there was Moorgate and the London to Penzance sleeper. The 1950s brought us Harrow and Doncaster. On 12 July 1913 it had been Colchester's turn to grieve. The GER Cromer to London Express had crashed into a lighter engine that had desperately tried to escape the scene. Its driver, spotting the Norfolk Coast Express bearing down upon him, had put on full steam in an attempt to get away. His heroic efforts were in vain. Fireman Keeble and driver Barnard were killed instantly. Guard Burdett received terrible injuries and died on the way to hospital. Two years later 150 died in a major crash near Gretna Green.

Above: Machinists and other workers from Hollington Brothers' clothing factory posed for this picture, not long before the outbreak of World War II. Largely a workforce of women, the raincoats and shirts they stitched would be accompanied by parachute silks and tunics when the balloon went up. The factory was one of the victims of the air raids, being bombed out during the war. In happier times the girls' fingers flew across the cloth, moving it and dragging it through the needles of the sewing machines. The speed and skill of their dexterity was a wonder to behold. The work could be boring, repeating the same task over and over again. That was where the good old 'Beeb' came in. Tannoys relayed radio's Light Programme into the workshops and rest rooms. The highlight of the day was Workers' Playtime. Popular singers and comics of the day performed in the studio and their acts brought a light relief to the monotony of the day. Up and coming comedians like Arthur Askey, with his welcome cry of 'Hello playmates', made the workforce chuckle. Some subjects were off limits, so no jokes were told about the Royal family, religion or body parts. Today's alternative comedians would not have stood a chance. Sandy Powell and Rob Wilton did not need to swear or use crude language to get a laugh. They were funny.

Above right: It is not just Americans who like to dress pretty girls in uniforms and send them out to be college football cheerleaders. Whilst these flowers of Essex beauty did not cavort like majorettes, they enjoyed dressing up and parading in mock military marching style. Known as the Holtona girls, they posed for this picture before setting off to take part in the 1937 town carnival. Their talents were not limited to their home town. The Holtona girls performed at other carnivals in Southend, Clacton, Chelmsford and Braintree. They were successful, too, as can be seen from the trophies and cups they won. Numbering around 100 strong, the girls from the factory of Hollington Brothers made an attractive and impressive sight. Many of them also enjoyed similar hobbies, in their spare time. There were troupes of Morris dancers who competed at other festivals. These were smaller groups, about 16 strong. They did not perform traditional folk dances like men's Morris dancing, but a style of formation and line dance. Dressed in short skirts and carrying pom-poms, this was the activity that reminded watchers of American majorettes. Competition was fierce as they battled for medals and ribbons. These were proudly pinned on their tunics and displayed at the next contest.

What a splendid sight to see the centre of Colchester's administration in all its glory. The town hall and Jumbo water tower are brightly illuminated as part of the Coronation celebrations for George VI. The nation had to wait until 12 May 1937 to hold its shindig. His father, George V, had died on 20 January 1936. In between times, there had been the abdication crisis when the heir apparent, Edward VIII, had announced his intention to wed the American divorcée, Wallis Simpson. Public and church opinion forced him into exile and his younger brother, real name Albert, assumed the monarchy on 11 December 1936. By the time coronation day came along, people were happy to forget the past and celebrate the future. The lights around the town hall could be glimpsed in Clacton and West Mersea. The first town hall had appeared following Colchester's first town charter of 1189. The Moot Hall, a Middle Ages name meaning 'courthouse', existed until it was destroyed in 1843. Three years later its successor was built, but only lasted to the end of the century. The present building, designed by John Belcher at a cost of £55,000, was opened in 1902.

There is not a single chance that this photograph was taken during the war years. Cries of 'turn that light out' or 'don't you know there is a war on?' would have had the air raid wardens turning purple with rage as they bellowed at those responsible. The Christmas lights illuminated Headgate, as the photographer pointed his lens along Crouch Street, out of St John's Street. Charles Clark and Son, at the Corner House, was a good place to get a stocking filler for dad or grandpa. Wills' Whiffs or a little packet of Manikin would keep the old man happy after lunch. For the seasoned pipe smoker, there was a plug of thick twist tobacco. It fascinated the kids to watch the old timer hewing at a hunk of the deep brown tobacco with his

sharp penknife. Then, it was rammed into the battered briar with a horny thumb and followed with the ritual lighting up ceremony. Only when the thick blue clouds of acrid smoke were billowing across the room was it time for him to join in the conversation. The bobbies on the corner were not tempted to slip inside the shop for a new pen. It looked like being a quiet night, with little to write a report about.

Events of the 1950s

HOT OFF THE PRESS

The 1950s seemed to be the heyday of spies, and in 1951 the activities of Guy Burgess and Donald Maclean caused a sensation in the country. Both had occupied prominent positions in the Foreign Office, while Burgess had also been a member of MI-6. Recruited by the Russians while at Cambridge University in the 1930s, the traitors provided the Soviets with a huge amount of valuable information. They disappeared in 1951, surfacing in Moscow five years later.

THE WORLD AT LARGE

Plans to develop the economies of member states into one common market came to fruition on 1st January 1958, when the EEC came into operation. The original members were France, Belgium, Luxembourg, The Netherlands, Italy, and West Germany. The Community became highly successful, achieving increased trade and prosperity across Western Europe while at the same time alleviating fear of war which lingered on after the end of World War II. Britain became a member in 1973.

SCIENCE AND DISCOVERY

DNA (deoxyribonucleic acid) was first defined as long ago as 1953, and the effects have been far-reaching. The key discovery was developed over the following years and today DNA fingerprinting has become an accepted part of life. Genetic diseases such as hemophilia and cystic fibrosis have been identified. Criminals are continually detected and brought to justice. Biological drugs have been developed. More controversially, drought and disease-resistant plants have been engineered - and Dolly the sheep has been produced.

Bottom: Saturday in the park and the deck chairs, forms and grass provide viewing spots for the afternoon's entertainment. Elsewhere in the world on 24 July 1943 there is excellent news about the progress of the war. On the eastern front, the Germans were on the run from the Red Army. Operation Barbarossa, the code name for the invasion of Russia, had failed. The tide had turned against the Axis powers. The Americans had captured Palermo and invaded the Italian mainland. When this audience woke up the next morning it was to discover that the Italian dictator, Mussolini, had resigned. Even as war raged on many fronts, there was still time to enjoy traditional entertainment in the park. Holly Trees (Castle Park) was alive with the laughter and cries of kiddies watching the Punch and Judy show. You could just make out the strains of music coming from the bandstand, but the sounds could not compete with the joyful noise of excited young children. Strings of sausages, battered wives and 'I say, I say, I say' style of policeman were the standard fare of the show. Not one child was traumatised by the mock violence, as po-faced do-gooders would have you believe today. The kids knew how to separate reality from make believe. That's the way to do it.

Right: The Corona Company carried out its business on St Peter's Street, on the northern side of the old Roman wall. Centre stage belongs to the staff of Luckin-Smith and Son. The ironmonger's shop on Head Street was part of a number of stores owned by Luckin-Smith that also sold groceries. The float is part of the Colchester carnival parade that would prove to

be one of the last of the town's celebrations before the outbreak of World War II. Pretty girls and dapper young men took a pride in their appearance as they drove through the town. Carefully garlanded, the attractive flowers and greenery made you glad to be English on a bright summer's day. People would be craning their necks as they lined the street, hoping to get a good look at the imaginatively decked floats. They were there to celebrate the strength of the community and to show a fierce pride in Colchester's traditional history and current success. Tradesmen and businesses sponsoring the procession were cute enough to make sure that the chance to get in some advertising did not go begging. Whilst asking you to support the local hospital seems to have been a charitable thought. Luckin-Smith made sure you knew that its paint saved your home just as well as hospital care saved you!

Oompah oompah and strike up the band. The marching brass is coming along High Street and passing the end of Museum Street and Maidenburgh Street. A newsagent's shop is sandwiched in between and, above the awning, members of the Conservative Club have a good view of the parade. The town carnival is getting off to a cheerful start on 19 July 1928. Women of the era were demonstrating new freedoms won by the Suffragettes. All women over 21 had just won the vote and their fashion kicked off the restraints imposed before the first world war. As recently as 1911, a woman had been arrested in London for wearing a split skirt, even though it was ankle length! Now young women were showing that they really did have legs. Everyday fashion saw skirts climb above the knee, short hair in vogue and slim young flappers setting new trends. Warning bells about the future were ringing, but not loudly enough. The American stock market fell 40 points, a large drop in those days. The massive Wall Street crash came the following year, wiping out businesses and private savings. Although times were hard after the war, this was one of the last carnival parades before the real years of depression gave a vicious bite.

Right: Look closely at the ranks of uniformed figures behind the snare drummer. Dressed like chocolate box toy soldiers, they are not really off to fight a war of yesteryear. They actually form a company drawn from the ranks of women employed at Hollington's clothing factory. They are not about to march off to a foreign shore, but to take part in the carnival parade. In the 1930s, these 'troops' were a regular feature of carnivals across Essex. As well as providing an entertainment for the workforce, they advertised the Hollington name to potential customers. The Holtona girls, as they were known, brightened up many a procession. Their uniforms were specially made in the factory. The wooden rifles they sloped had little bike reflectors placed in the muzzles. These glinted in the light, pretending to be gun flashes. The management took the company seriously. The girls were not just allowed to look smart and cute. They had to march properly. A retired army captain drilled the machinists as rigorously as any sergeant major at Colchester barracks. Did these volunteers realise that their husbands and sweethearts would don uniforms for real within a few short years? Real rifles would be spitting fire, not just reflecting the sunshine.

Below: 'Stupid boy.' How TV audiences of the 1970s laughed when Captain Mainwaring grumbled at the young Private Pike in the sitcom 'Dad's Army'. The programme was so successful that repeats were still being televised long after most of the cast had died. The exploits of the Home Guard on the small screen were hilarious. In real life they were deadly serious. Many old timers were offended by the way they had been portrayed. Drawn from the ranks of those too old to be called up, too unfit to see active service or in reserved occupations, they volunteered to do their bit. Had the enemy landed he would have been faced with a brave bunch of men willing to fight to the last drop of blood, however outclassed they might have been. Originally the Land Defence Volunteers, the name was changed at Churchill's suggestion in 1940. This 1944 group, with JL Pye centre front of the name plate, was arranged outside the EN Mason factory on Cowdray Avenue. This new factory, the Arclight Works, opened the previous year. Its earlier building had been damaged in the air raid of October 1942. Mrs Mason had founded the company in 1905, before handing over to her son, Bernard. It made office equipment and pioneered photocopying materials. Aeroplanes on reconnaissance missions used its inks and photographic paper.

Above: Whilst not suffering the major bombing raids that hit the big cities in the 1940s, Colchester was in a constant state of alert for the day when its turn came. Already hit a number of times during the war, residents could sense something of the pain and suffering that London, Liverpool, Birmingham and Coventry had undergone when the incendiaries rained down on St Botolph's Corner in the early hours of Wednesday 23 February 1944. Bloomfield and Company's furniture business was gutted. It relocated to premises under the Liberal Club at Headgate. Life had to go on. Behind it, Kavanagh's boot and shoe factory has suffered a similar fate. This business, like so many, had started out as a one man affair, growing gradually into becoming a major employer. John Kavanagh had begun it all in the 19th century when he took on the repair of army boots and the renovation of

those that had been rejected. These were resold as well as resoled at a good profit. He took factory space in part of St Botolph's brewery in Stanwell Street. When the site was badly damaged by fire in 1889, there were 300 on the payroll, supplying nine London shops. The new, electrically lit factory was opened in 1892 and stood until the bombers flew in.

Top: The sandbags are piled against the foot of the town hall. Although not directly targeted by the Luftwaffe, Colchester lay on the flight path of the bombers carrying their deadly loads towards London. It did not take much of a miscalculation to unleash a hail of death upon the town below. The sandbags might help to soften the blow, but Colcestrians did not want the theory to be tested. Walking alongside the town hall, the man in the picture may be about to enter the Cups Hotel. Built in 1701, it was named after the drinking vessel of the age that gave rise to the expression 'to be in his cups'. That term for being drunk has been replaced by more modern and far ruder expressions that cannot be mentioned here! The three cups that adorned the building referred to the Worshipful Company of Salters. One of Colchester's top hotels, its bus met every train in the 1860s and the Royal Mail coach called every night on its way to the capital. Admiral Nelson and Lady Hamilton once had a lovers' tryst here. A new sign, five feet across and weighing six hundredweight, was erected in 1959. It closed in 1965, but a new Cups opened on Trinity Street in 1977. The building had to be strengthened to carry the weight of the sign that was transferred from the old building.

Scheregate leads north from St John's Street towards Sir Isaac's Walk. The Roman wall ran across Scheregate, from east to west. The southern postern gate in the town walls was situated here. A forlorn advert for Fyffes' bananas appears in the window above the bicycle. It was be a long time before that fruit returned as part of the British diet. A generation of children grew up only knowing a banana from pictures they had seen. The soldiers are heading off towards one of the air raid shelters that became part of life in the early 40s. Anderson shelters, named after the government minister, were built to give some protection from German bombs. When the sirens went, people grabbed blankets and flasks of soup and settled down for an uncomfortable night.

Better that than being trapped in a bombed out house. Later in the war, the minister for home security, Herbert Morrison, would have an indoor shelter named after him. It was more of a reinforced table than anything and did not inspire a great deal of confidence. The soldiers remind us that Colchester is Britain's oldest garrison town. The first barracks were built in 1794 and a permanent garrison established in 1856, during the Crimean War.

Events of the 1950s

MELODY MAKERS

Few teenage girls could resist the blatant sex-appeal of 'Elvis the Pelvis', though their parents were scandalised at the moody Presley's provocatively gyrating hips. The singer took America and Britain by storm with such hits as 'Jailhouse Rock', 'All Shook Up' and 'Blue Suede Shoes'. The rhythms of Bill Haley and his Comets, Buddy Holly and Chuck Berry turned the 1950s into the Rock 'n' Roll years.

INVENTION AND TECHNOLOGY

Until the late 1950s you did not carry radios around with you. Radios were listened to at home, plugged into a mains socket in every average sitting room. Japan was in the forefront of electronic developments even then, and in 1957 the Japanese company Sony introduced the world's very first all-transistor radio - an item of new technology that was small enough to fit into your pocket. The major consumer product caught on fast - particularly with teenage listeners.

ROYAL WATCH

King George VI's health had been causing problems since 1948, when he developed thrombosis. In 1951 the King - always a heavy smoker - became ill again, and was eventually found to be suffering from lung cancer. His left lung was removed in September of 1951. In January 1952 he waved Princess Elizabeth and Prince Philip off on their tour of Africa; they were never to see him again. The King died in the early hours of 6th February 1952.

Above: High Street was a two way thoroughfare when this photo was taken. The emergency water tanks are just one sign of the war years that we came to accept as normal on our streets. Two magnificent buildings dominate this part of town. The Grand Theatre or Hippodrome helped keep up our spirits during the gloomy years. We could forget the dark skies for a few hours when Stanley Holloway entertained us or that cheeky chappie, Max Miller, made us laugh. We loved to be shocked by the jokes from his blue book. They would seem tame, now. After the show, we slipped next door. The pub had been serving ale as the Lamb since 1778. Bought by the Colchester Brewing Company in 1886, it was demolished in 1905, but was reborn as a building of similar style to the town hall. New owners, Ind Coope, changed it to the Bay and Stay in 1971, spending £20,000 on a refit. The old Lamb had developed an unsavoury reputation as a bit of a roughhouse, but the alterations seemed to have little effect. Recalled the Lamb Inn or the Lamb Alehouse, from 1994 it has tried to revert to being an old style pub to try to recapture its former glory.

Above right: Any royal visit is a special occasion. When the reigning monarch comes to call, it is an honour. Best uniforms and medals come out of mothballs and local bigwigs have something to tell their grandchildren about. The privilege of greeting the Queen personally is one granted to a small few. In 1958, when she called into our town, the townspeople turned out in force. The pavements were packed with hordes straining to get a glimpse of the woman who was one of the most popular figures in the land. They waved little Union Jacks on sticks and cheered as the royal car swung down the street. The cynical days of criticism of the marital doings of her children were some years away. It was only five years before that we had watched the flickering black and white TV pictures from Westminster Abbey. As Richard Dimbleby commentated, we all shared the pride of the nation as the Archbishop of Canterbury lowered the crown onto her head. She was a symbol of what we saw to be good about Britain. Queen Elizabeth II of Britain and the Commonwealth she might be, but she could relate to ordinary folk. Here she was, carrying a handbag just like any woman. She was also a mum, with two children, and we knew all about being a parent.

Shopping spree

Griffin's furniture store and removal service has long gone from here. There is a large roundabout in the place of most of the buildings. Depending upon his age, a local will know this spot as St Botolph's Corner, St Botolph's Circus or Plough Corner. The last of these names provides a link with the pub that once stood here. The Plough had a typical Georgian style frontage built onto an older timber framed structure. A Dunthorne painting from 1783 showed it well. One of the first of the pub's signs was made from an old working plough. Sadly, that disappeared many years ago. It was claimed that beer was brewed there back in 1732. There was plenty of beer around, over the years. In 1900, three innkeepers were hauled before 'the beak'. They were accused of allowing drunkenness in the Railway Tavern, the Fountain and the Plough; pubs all close to each other. The milk float in the picture could have provided the drinkers with a healthier pinta. The Plough had some real characters as landlords. Freddie Bird was one such notable licensee. He was a comedian and loved to entertain his customers with comic ditties. Some of these became even funnier, depending upon how much ale had been supped. The Plough served its last pint in 1969.

Events of the 1960s

WHAT'S ON?
Television comedy came into its own in the 1960s, and many of the shows that were favourites then went on to become classics. 'On the Buses', 'Steptoe and Son', 'Till Death Us Do Part' and 'The Army Game' kept audiences laughing, while the incredible talents of Morecambe and Wise, the wit of Des O'Connor - often the butt of the duo's jokes - and the antics of Benny Hill established them for ever in the nation's affections.

GETTING AROUND
The 2nd March 1969 was a landmark in the history of aviation. The Anglo-French supersonic airliner Concorde took off for the first time from Toulouse in France. Concorde, which can cruise at almost twice the speed of sound, was designed to fly from London to New York in an incredible three hours twenty minutes. The event took place just weeks after the Boeing 747, which can carry 500 passengers to Concorde's modest 100, made its first flight.

SPORTING CHANCE
Wembley Stadium saw scenes of jubilation when on 30th July 1966 England beat West Germany 4-2 in the World Cup. The match, played in a mixture of sunshine and showers, had been a nailbiting experience for players and spectators alike from the very beginning when Germany scored only thirteen minutes into the game. It was Geoff Hurst's two dramatic goals scored in extra time that secured the victory and lifted the cup for England - at last.

Headgear was a dead give-away in the early 40s. Most men went into town in a suit or jacket and trousers. But, the 'titfer' was different. Working classes wore their caps with pride. The middle classes had to be that little cut above and sported trilbies, homburgs or even bowlers. The dapper chap on the right has just come out of the newsagency. He has a military bearing. The ramrod spine suggests an army career. Did he take the billboard at

its word? It asked him to give the newsagent a standing order! The cyclist is making good use of the baskets and bags on her bike. She has got her weekly ration and is well loaded down as she heads off along Crouch Street, following the line of the Roman wall, on which these shops back. Meaning 'cross', Crouch Street gets its name from the church and hospital of the 'crouched' or 'crutched' friars that was founded in 1244 on the south side of the street. Our cyclist is well protected from the elements with her felt hat pulled firmly down and her long coat modestly covering her lower limbs. Let us hope her coat did not catch in the chain or she would have wished that the nursing talents of the friars had not disappeared.

Above: These shops are on the east side of Head Street. The entrance to Culver Street is in between the Tudor Café and the Forsdike and Bonner grocery shop. As the woman passed AJ Clamp's tobacconist shop, her nostrils were twitching from taking in the aroma of old shag from one display and the scent of coffee beans from the next. On this day in May 1934, the bus was moving towards Headgate. It had no competition on the streets. Public transport had undergone an upheaval in the 1920s. After over a decade of planning, a tramway system had opened in 1904 with a fleet of 16 trams. The trams' lack of flexibility on the roads and the increasing congestion they caused with the growing car population caused a rethink on their use. A 1927 Corporation Act paved the way for the abandonment of the tram. The following year, buses appeared on the streets and, by 1929, the clanking stopped. The last one ran on 8th December. The quiet state of the road, not a car in sight and just a couple of cyclists easing their way southward, suggests that the town was not as congested as stated. However, by this time, the bypass had opened and much of the through traffic had been diverted.

Below: This building was known as the telegraph office. It later became the Eastern Electricity Centre. In 1954, as 38 Head Street, it was home to Powell and Coates, the travel agents. The customers outside the shop might have been discussing their next holiday. A simple run down the coast to Clacton or Southend was common enough, but the British tourist was soon to be spreading her wings a little bit further. She had more money in her purse as the wartime days of austerity were being left behind. The ceremonial burning of ration books took place in July when restrictions on meat, the last item to go, were finally lifted. Lester Piggott, a mere 18 year old, rode the Derby winner and Roger Bannister ran a sub four minute mile. It was a year to do something new. A fortnight across the water in the Isle of Wight or the Channel Islands was possible. Alternatively, a couple of weeks revisiting the Normandy beaches for their soldier husbands were adventures that had been the privilege of the well off a few years ago. Horizons were being widened and ordinary people applied for passports for the first time. Whilst many of us saw no further than Butlin's, the more intrepid booked for Brittany or the Adriatic.

Below: Everyone knows that the M & S store is a sure place for quality and keen pricing. So established has it become that the full name of the shop is seldom used. Throughout most of the 20th century shoppers have come to rely on the St Michael brand, from the patron saint of underwear. Rows of skirts, jumpers and blouses sit alongside the children's wear. Many's the time you've been kitted out for the new school year in a Marks & Spencer grey shirt, blue jersey and pleated skirt. Well, you would have been if you were a girl, but who knows these days? The building on High Street owed thanks to

Michael Marks, the man who started his penny bazaar on a Leeds market stall in 1884. He joined forces with Thomas Spencer in 1894 and the business grew into one of the best loved shopping experiences in Britain. Any visitor to a strange town, looking to spend a couple of hours happily shopping, will always ask where she can find the nearest 'Marks and Sparks'. As the 21st century began, change was afoot in the empire. Shrinking profits and fierce competition from supermarkets, that expanded their reach into traditional M & S country, forced the company to rethink its approach. Traditional suppliers were dropped and new ranges, like Agent Provocateur lingerie, were introduced.

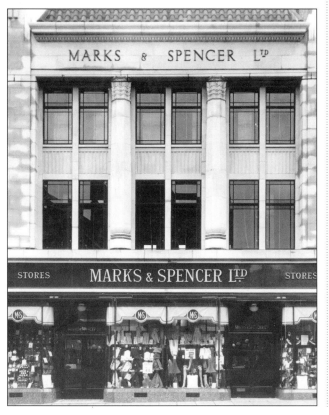

Bottom: A largely deserted Head Street, with the shops of F Luckin-Smith and the Colchester Gas Company on its west side, is pictured stretching off towards North Hill. At such a quiet time, before the streets sprang into life, it was a chance to recall the way Colchester had developed. From Norman times, the town had relied heavily on its market, fishery and cloth industries. The disruptions of the 17th century civil war had caused upset when the town was under siege for 11 weeks. It was ironic that Cromwell's forces starved the population into submission as the town had supported the government, only to be captured by Royalists. After those events, life returned to normal. It was the coming of the railway that opened up wider trading possibilities. The engineering industry was developed and local events, like the Oyster Feast, became national events. Visitors rediscovered Colchester's past and Essex's cultural capital regained some of its old importance. Shops and businesses, such as these on Head Street, flourished in the late 19th and 20th centuries. By the time the new millennium dawned, engineering still featured as an important source of revenue. However, the largest influence on the Colchester economy comes from service industries.

This is the west side of Head Street. The photographer has captured a view leading north from Headgate, at the junction with St John's Street where the old Roman wall crossed Head Street. On the left, Church Street divides Halford's cycle shop from Thorogood's. Turning down Church Street would bring you to the Church of St Mary at the Walls. Gutted in 1648 during the 76 day siege of Colchester, it had been a Royalist stronghold during the civil war. WJ Thorogood was a pastry cook and this establishment was both a shop and restaurant. The smell of freshly baked almond slices, maids of honour and sugary doughnuts made mouths water as the aromas wafted across the pavement. Shops like that never needed much in the way of advertising to attract

Events of the 1960s

HOT OFF THE PRESS

Barbed wire, concrete blocks and a wide no-man's-land divided East from West when a reinforced wall was built right across the city of Berlin in 1961. Many East Germans escaped to the West at the eleventh hour, taking with them only the possessions they could carry. The Berlin Wall divided the city - and hundreds of family members and friends - for 28 years until the collapse of Communist rule across Eastern Europe. Who can ever forget those scenes in 1989, when ordinary people themselves began to physically tear down the hated wall?

THE WORLD AT LARGE

'One giant leap for mankind' was taken on 20th July 1969, when Neil Armstrong made history as the first man to set foot on the moon. During the mission he and fellow-astronaut 'Buzz' Aldrin collected rock and soil samples, conducted scientific experiments - and had a lot of fun jumping around in the one-sixth gravity. Twenty-one hours and thirty-seven minutes after their landing they took off again in their lunar module 'Eagle' to rejoin Apollo II which was orbiting above them, proudly leaving the American flag on the Moon's surface.

ROYAL WATCH

Princess Margaret's announcement in 1960 that she was to wed photographer Antony Armstrong-Jones (later Lord Snowdon) brought sighs of relief from her immediate family. Just five years earlier the people of Britain had sympathised as the princess bowed to public and private pressure, ending her relationship with Peter Townsend, Prince Philip's former equerry. The Church (and the Queen, as its Head) frowned on the liaison as Townsend was divorced. Her marriage to Lord Snowdon itself ended in 1978.

custom. The warm smell of crusty bread, the pungent tang of roasted coffee beans and the mystical charms conjured up by Turkish tobacco had their individual appeal. Some customers of those shopkeepers indulged in nose shopping rather than window gazing. Even so, it was difficult to resist the temptation to enter and buy half a pound of arabica, an ounce of Balkan sobranie or one of Thorogood's tasty pies.

Prices in Kay's, on Long Wyre Street, were clearly marked in shillings and pence. Children, before 1971, had to work out the cost of 37 items priced at £4 15s 7d each. Quite why, it is not certain, but they could. Who ever bought 37 of anything? It was never questioned. Armed with the knowledge that 12d made a shilling and 20s made a pound, they long multiplied and produced the answer. Today, the shop assistant needs a calculator to total three 25p sweet bars. The delivery boy had plenty to do, as well as mathematics. He had to wash the floor, donkey-stone

The delivery boy not only delivered the groceries, he washed the floor and donkey-stoned the step

the step and then load up the basket on his bike with the grocery order. When he arrived at his destination he would be expected to collect the money from the housewife and give her the right change. The calculations were done in his head and not with the help of any electronic aid. He had another unwritten job to perform. He was the acid test for the new pop songs of the day. Hear him whistling one, it was going to be a hit. In case the reader went to school in the last 30 years, the answer you have tried to work out is £176 16s 7d.

Below: Allen and Son, towards the right, was a long established butcher. It served shoppers on St Botolph's Street for around 80 years. How many chops were chopped or pounds of mince minced in that time? Further up the street, the Victorian building stands out. It was put up after a large fire had destroyed that part of the street. St Botolph's Street led to St Botolph's Gate that stood until 1817. The shop this side of Allen's sold illustrated local guides. Colchester has long been a place that attracted visitors. Its Roman connections, Norman castle and oyster industry brought people from home and abroad to soak up the history and sample the delicacies. The guidebook shop did good business. Sadly, there were few welcome guests in 1940. Herr Hitler sent some of his friends in the Luftwaffe to visit, but they were not interested in the town's heritage. The pilots of Junkers aircraft wanted to provide more ruins. We already had one famous one of our own. The priory, after which this street was named, had its origins dating back 1,000 years. Then, there was just a small parish church and community of priests. But, around 1100, work was begun on the first religious house in England to follow the rule of St Augustine. The priory of St Julian and St Botolph began to take shape.

Bottom: In the summer of 1935 there were street parties to celebrate the silver jubilee of George V. The dark days of depression were left behind as unemployment fell by over a third from the 3,000,000 high of 1932. Sports fixtures attracted record crowds and the beaches were filled with holidaymakers who had money to burn. By the look of this picture, the bobby on point duty was having an easy time of it. Most of the town seems to have gone off to the seaside. This corner of High Street, with Head Street running down to the left, had been subject to improvement to help the traffic flow. It was not to be tested on this day. Colchester's contribution to Jesse Boot's chain of chemist shops held a prime position on the southeast corner. Every town now has one of his stores that developed from the humble chemist shop, with its simple range of medicines, to an institution on every high street. A range of perfumes, toiletries and beauty aids was added. It could have been called the 'sweet smell of success'. He became well loved for his charity work. Jesse Boot gave away much of his fortune. His home town of Nottingham benefited from his benevolence. Jesse's efforts were rewarded when he became Lord Trent. He died in 1931.

The impressive Co-op building occupies the corner of Long Wyre Street and Culver Street. The first fully organised Co-op had been set up in 1844, by the Rochdale Society of Equitable Pioneers. The society created a set of organisational and working rules that were widely adopted. They included open membership, democratic control, no religious or political discrimination, sales at prevailing market prices and the setting aside of some earnings for education. The Rochdale Co-op opened in a little shop in Toad Lane. By 1861 the ideas that had begun up north had rapidly spread across the country. In Colchester, a meeting in Thompson's coffee house on Wyre Street looked at a copy of Rochdale's rules. This was followed by a general meeting in the public hall. Excited by the new

approach to retailing, the first business premises were rented on Culver Street. At a cost of £18 per annum, the Co-op was launched. Its very first purchases were two pecks of bread. The shop opened from 7 am until 9 pm. By 1877 it was doing so well that the Culver Street outlet concentrated on grocery and bakery. Further premises on Long Wyre Street were bought for £1,225 to deal in drapery and shoes. Sales had risen to £9,733 for the year. The Co-op flourished.

Events of the 1960s

MELODY MAKERS
The 1960s: those were the days when the talented blues guitarist Jimi Hendrix shot to rock stardom, a youthful Cliff Richard charmed the nation with his 'Congratulations' and Sandie Shaw won the Eurovision Song Contest for Britain with 'Puppet on a String'. It was the combined musical talents of a group of outrageous working-class Liverpool lads, however, who formed the Beatles and took the world by storm with music that ranged from the experimental to ballads such as 'Yesterday'.

INVENTION AND TECHNOLOGY
A major step forward was made in 1960 when the laser was invented. An acronym for Light Amplification by Stimulated Emission of Radiation, the device produces a narrow beam of light that can travel for vast distances and is focused to give enormous power. Laser beams, as well as being able to carry far more information than radio waves, can also be used for surgery, cutting, drilling, welding and scores of other operations.

SCIENCE AND DISCOVERY
When the drug Thalidomide was first developed during the 1950s it was hailed as a wonder drug which would ease the distressing symptoms of pregnancy sickness. By the early 1960s the drug's terrible side effects were being discovered, when more than 3000 babies had been born with severe birth defects. Malformed limbs, defective eyes and faulty intestines were the heart-rending legacy left by Thalidomide.

Above: High Street boasts a history of architecture. The house above the group of shop awnings dates back to medieval times. Its double jetted structure was hidden behind a 19th century facade. To the right, the George had similar medieval origins and its frontage had a 18th century covering. In bygone days this street was quite simply referred to as 'the market'. A cattle market was held along here until 1859. Locals sometimes refer to it as a cattle market now, as they push and shove their way along the pavements on a busy Saturday afternoon's shopping expedition. The east end was known as Cornhill as long ago as 1336. Even further along was called Frere (Friar) Street. The first reference to the whole length of the road as High Street was made in 1470, though it was much later when this became the name in general use. Babyland would not do good business for some time. The birth rate fell during the war as loved ones lived their lives apart from one another. It was not surprising to see the baby boom years of the late 1940s come along. Men returned from active duty overseas and resumed another form of active duty at home. Prospective grannies started to knit little woolly coats once more.

Above right: Crossing High Street towards East Stockwell Street, these two housewives are unlikely to be on their way to Claridge and Company. They are hardly likely to be having their tennis racquets restrung. Somehow they do not look the sort to be apeing the play of the great Helen Wills Moody who dominated Wimbledon in the pre-war years. That shop is now Red Lion books and would have been more likely to get their custom if it had been there in 1940. Robinson's chemist shop traded next door and, further along, Babyland offered little bootees and mittens for their grand-children. Walking in perfect step with one another, they belong to an age when women went out well wrapped up, whatever the weather. Ladies wore hats in public and long coats, almost to the floor. They might have been thinking about the war of 1914-18 in which their husbands had fought. Having survived the horrors of that conflict, they now had to endure the pain of seeing their sons march off to another that was supposed to end all wars. Headed for East Stockwell Street, named after the spring that had once been there, the Dutch quarter lay behind the outfitter's. To get there they would have to walk down the street that used to be called Bear Lane, after a pub that stood there.

Short Wyre Street is not short of shoppers on this day in 1940. We do not know whether they had money to burn at Bonner's jewellery shop, on the right down towards Eld Lane (once Old Lane), or were looking for a bargain at Hilton's shoe shop or Foster's clothiers. What is known, as we look from the corner with Queen Street, is that the menfolk could have nipped into the Little Crown for a quick pint while the women got on with it. The male of the species is nothing if not predictable. 'I'll pop in here, love, so as not to get under your feet and let you get on with it.' Typical! But, at least, he wouldn't be a nuisance with his continual moaning about how long we were taking. Hubby could get some history with his drink. The Little Crown was a small pub rather than a small crown. Formerly the Crown Beer Shop, it dated from 1855 and existed as a beer shop until 1951, when it was granted a full license. As one of the town's last beer houses, it had a wild west flavour with its sawdust and old time feel. The Little Crown has a magnificent Victorian fireplace as its centrepiece.

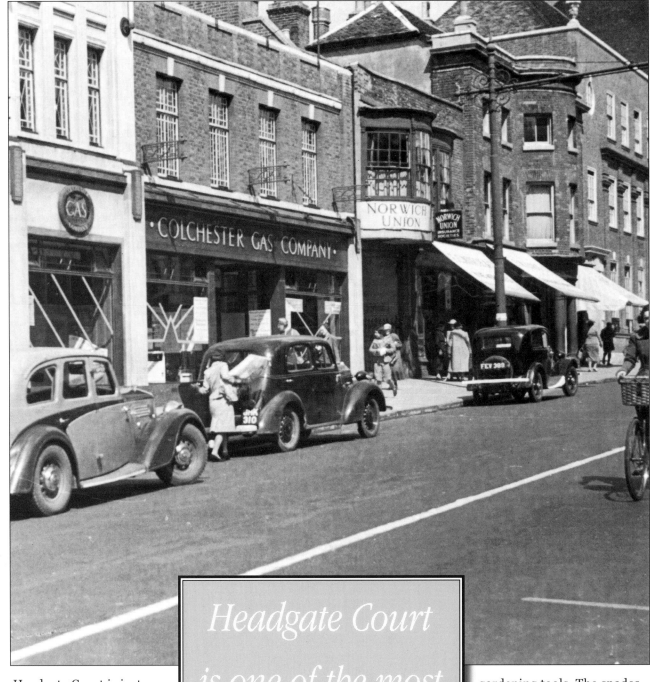

Headgate Court is just a modestly sized area leading off Head Street. The entry to it is in between the Colchester Gas Company and Norwich Union buildings. Hidden away from this camera shot, it is one of the important sites in the history of the town. It was here, in 1648, that the civil war siege document was signed, bringing to an end the 76 days of hardship that Colchester had suffered. The Luckin-Smith shop was but one of many in the 1940s that were dotted across the region. Many were part of a grocery chain that also included ironmongery and

Headgate Court is one of the most important sites in the history of the town

gardening tools. The spades and hoes being advertised in 1940 would be used for more than a hobby in the years to follow. They became part of the war effort. Back lawns were tilled and waste land turned into allotments as the nation dug for victory. Lawn mowers disappeared into sheds and seed drills were drawn into the land that would support vegetables to see us through the winter. Occasionally, the hoes would double as rifles when the Home Guard practised its manoeuvres and sloped arms. Real weapons were not available for every volunteer. They were needed at the front.

At work

Arcadia was an amusement 'arcade' that encouraged you to meet your friends there. This was not an age of space invader machines and shoot 'em up computer games. Here you could play simple fruit machines and pintables. Jacklin's café, up above, was the place to eat. Even in the 1980s it had a certain style. Staff dressed in the costume of the 1930s, giving it a refined 'Oxford and Cambridge' feel. It only closed in the mid 1990s. It is now the site of Williams and Griffin department store. The Cups Hotel, along to the right, had some of its best years during the Napoleonic Wars. The Earl of Onslow sumptuously entertained his fellow officers of the Surrey Fencible Dragoons here in 1794. Admiral Duncan was a visitor in 1799, followed by the Danish and Turkish ambassadors. The Princess of Monaco gave the Cups a royal status when she stayed in the hotel in 1802. There is no record of her having visited the Arcadia, however. She was probably more at home on the croquet lawn than in trying to get three cherries in a line or avoiding a tilt message as she flicked the flippers as a pinball wizard.

Teamwork, learned in the classroom sticking lumps of papier-maché together to make little models, is seen again in the town planner's office. The last touches are being put to the relief model of the Colchester bypass. It had become essential to reroute the through traffic out of the town centre. At the beginning of the 1930s, the planners were keen to give the bypass a touch of class, as well as being an effective means of improving traffic flow. The western stretch was called Cymbeline Way, marking the historical links with the king immortalised in Shakespeare's romantic play. The course of the bypass lies across the site of Camulodunum, by Sheepen Farm. Work on the road was preceded by careful excavation of the area. Evidence of the importance of the pre-Roman settlement was uncovered. This helped further the reputation of the Castle Museum. All sorts of artefacts and remains had been unearthed around this time. The excavation of the Balkerne Gate in 1917, the discovery of Roman houses in Castle Park in 1920, the tumulus in Lexden in 1924 and the temple in Holly Trees meadow in 1928 all added to the historical importance that Colchester wanted to advertise to the world. Just to be awkward, locals stubbornly referred to Cymbeline Way as 'the bypass', but were proud of its heritage, nonetheless.

> *The western stretch of the bypass was named Cymbeline Way, marking the historical links with Shakespeare's king*

Keeping time - Rose of Colchester

George Rose was working as an almanac salesman, learning all aspects of the trade, when he decided to use the experience he had gathered during this time to establish his own business. At the beginning of the 20th century, in 1908, George's ambitions were realised and he founded his own calendar (or almanac as they were called then) manufacturing business in Colchester. The company was founded under the name E Rose and Co and marked the beginning of the long-lasting family business which is known today as Rose of Colchester Ltd.

A typical early almanac from the company's archives is for the year 1913, for John Jones, a Merchant Tailor. This almanac was just one length of paper with a large photograph, print advertising John Jones and a surprisingly small concentration on the actual dates of the year! However, using advertising as the main purpose of the almanacs proved to be a successful direction for George's company and indeed, helped to ensure its enduring success.

Colchester's Kendall Road became the long lasting site of E Rose and Co's first factory and was to become the company home for some 77 years. In the early days illustrations were monochrome, and adverts were composed using Founders Type in case. When colour was introduced, illustrations for the calendars were printed by four colour letterpress on a single flatbed Heidelberg. Adverts were

printed by letterpress platens on headboards which were stitched to the calendar pages.

This success was to continue as George's company expanded throughout the next three decades. However, the advent of the second world war brought with it a slight pause to the rapid progression of the company. During the period from 1939 to 1945 there was a shortage of paper. This, combined with the rationing taking place at the time, inevitably restricted the output from the Kendall Road factory. To add to this hindrance, punitive rates of Purchase Tax were later imposed on calendars causing a further obstacle for the company.

However, in 1945 when Ivor Rose, George Rose's nephew, took over, these obstacles were overcome and Rose of Colchester put the war years behind them. Indeed, just over a decade after the end of the second world war, in 1956, Rose of Colchester was able to form a Limited Company.

The 24th February, 1962 was a day marked with misfortune for the calendar manufacturers. The Kendall Road factory, which was by then embarking on its second half century, suffered a fire. This fire seriously damaged the

Above centre:
The company's first almanac, produced for John Jones in 1913.
Right: *An image used on an early calendar.*

COBBLER STICK TO YOUR LAST.

factory which subsequently had to be repaired. Only three years after this setback another serious threat was posed to the prosperity of the company. In 1965 a government bill put the nature of the calendar manufacturing business in to question. The Finance Bill (No 2), clause 14 stated that the production of calendars was classified as business entertainment. Once again the Rose family were forced to battle against the odds for the survival of their business. They proceeded to send calendars to several MP's and eventually proved that their products were for advertising purposes rather than merely for business entertainment!

After 77 years of service from the Kendall Road factory for Rose of Colchester, the business parted company with the old premises in 1986. Importantly, for a family business such as Rose of Colchester, their new and improved factory in Clough Road at Severalls Industrial Park maintained their firmly rooted base in the local area. The equipment and methods of production used by this time were fully modernised and a marked contrast to the materials George Rose was forced to cope with in the beginning. Now, a five colour sheet-fed Litho process is used running at 10,000 sheets per hour on a double day shift using the latest computer-generated origination as well as a direct-to-plate system for overprinting adverts and four Wiro binding machines used to finish the calendar with adverts printed on each sheet.

Above: *The company won the National Business Calendar Awards in 1997.*
Top: *The company's first premises at Kendall Road.*

The new Clough Road factory brought further success for the Rose of Colchester company which led them into their ninth successful decade of business. In 1997, the quality of Rose of Colchester's success was acknowledged when they won a National Business Calendar Award. Only a year later this success became visible when the construction of a new building, completed in 1998, extended the factory site at Clough Road.

This flourishing business has been passed down through the Rose family generations. Ivor Frederick Rose was the next Rose to join the company after George. He took on the role of Managing Director until his death in 1981 when Christopher George Rose replaced him whilst working as a Production Director. Currently, Edward Richard Rose acts as the Chairman of the company. Finally, when Michael David Rose joined the company in 1991 as Production and Publicity Director he became the fourth Rose generation to contribute to what truly is a family business. Today, with a staff of 45 and 90 selling agents, Rose of Colchester continues to provide a high quality service to its customers. Their main markets are the manufacturing and service industries as well as sole traders throughout the UK. However, they also manufacture calendars for companies in the Irish Republic and even for companies as far away as Africa. The company's unique selling points include the range of original and attractive designs as well as the value for money that their calendars offer. In celebration of the year 2000, to mark the Millennium, the company have produced several special calendars to add to their usual range including titles such as, 'Time', 'The Way We Were' and 'A Century Of Transport'. Through their investment of profits back in to the business the Rose family are hoping to continue the tradition of expansion into the 21st century by cornering more of the calendar market.

Above: Part of the range of Millennium calendars produced by the company.
Below: An aerial view of the Clough Road premises today.

Warming to success

In the early part of the twentieth century, in the midst of the 'roaring twenties', two men of vision, Charles H Lindsey and his son Charles R Lindsey, decided to set up a business in Colchester to specialise in the design and installation of all kinds of heating, ventilating and hot water systems.

(50p) a week plus whatever he could earn by overtime and his extra efforts. His apprenticeship completed, Charles senior spent some years working in London gaining wide experience in what were then considered the newest and most revolutionary types of heating and ventilating systems.

Though the 1920s may have been 'roaring' for some, those were still relatively hard times for the man in the street, the country was still painfully climbing out of the trough of World War I, and it took courage and initiative to branch out into business on one's own. But both men had a solid core of experience in the trade to give them confidence.

Charles senior had been apprenticed in 1890 to Alfred Bowsher, plumber and hot water fitter of Lenham, near Maidstone in Kent. His indentures, hand-written on parchment, are still in the possession of his family, and record that the first year he was to receive no wages, the second year he could take home 3 shillings (15p) a week, the third year six shillings (30p) and thereafter 10 shillings

Came 1914 and the Great War, and he brought his family to Colchester where he joined the firm of Williams & Co in High Street. Charles junior, joined his father as an apprentice with Williams & Co in 1916. By the mid-1920s it was time to branch out, and the two Charles set up business at Bombay Cottage, 55 Harwich Road, Colchester.

Their first form of transport was a bicycle with a large carrier, but it soon became apparent that the accoutrements

Above left: *Charles Lindsey, who together with his son, Charles junior, founded the company.*
Above right: *An early letterhead.*
Below: *Workforce at Maldon Grammar School 1935.*

the coach house, stables and harness room which for many years had housed the horse-dawn Royal Mail.

The year 1926 went down in history as that of the miners' strike and the general strike. Morale everywhere was low, and all businesses felt the pinch. For the Lindseys it was the first taste of those inevitable difficulties which every firm worth its salt feels many times over the years of trading. Contracts were cancelled because of the general feeling of uncertainty and difficulty in obtaining raw materials and only by their own spirit and the loyalty and hard work of the staff they had now begun to gather round them, did Lindseys weather the storm.

The post-1926 period was significant in the heating and ventilating industry because the lack of solid fuel precipitated a changeover to oil, then a very revolutionary concept. Lindseys as always were in the van of progress, and were soon deeply involved with the new type of fuel. They received numerous enquiries and orders for installations and a happy and busy period ensued. And oil was 4d (2p) a gallon!

of a heating and ventilating expert required greater capacity than that provided by a bicycle. So the new firm purchased a hand-cart, admittedly slightly past its best. But diligent repairs, a fine coat of paint and the firm's name emblazoned handsomely on the side soon made it a vehicle to be proud of - an admirable combination of transport and advertising medium in the best modern tradition of the day.

Because the passage-way from road to workshop was so narrow the hand-cart had to be dismantled and re-assembled every time it was used. This created much entertainment and delight for the neighbours. Charles junior recalled that the consequent embarrassment so improved their speed and agility that they might have rivalled the Gunners who put on such impressive displays of gun dismantling at military tattoos!

This delightful state of affairs lasted barely a year, for in 1926 the Lindseys took their handcart and their business to East Stockwell Street, Colchester, where they set up home in

Booming again, C H Lindsey and Son greatly expanded their operations and always with a careful eye to the future, put a great deal of effort into recruiting and training staff to meet the high standards expected and the improvements taking place within the heating and ventilating industry.

The old hand-cart was still giving sterling service, but such was business that heavy and bulky materials were transported by hired horse and cart. Even in those compara-

Above left: *Charles Lindsey senior enjoying a 'happy hour' with some of his craftsmen.* ***Top:*** *Workforce at Wivenhoe Shipyard during the war years.*

tively leisurely days the early bird caught the worm, or in this case, the contract, and to improve communications with clients not readily served by public transport, a second-hand car was purchased for £88. This car, a 1923 bull-nose Morris Oxford with Hotchkiss engine and with a handsome dickey seat with its own windscreen, came to a sad and untimely end on the road to Wrabness. Young Charles was driving. His father wearing his customary bowler hat, was beside him, while two fitters sat in the dickey seat.

However, the driver of an approaching steam lorry owned by the old East Anglian Roastone Company, failed to observe this dignified entourage until it was too late and, despite young Charles' desperate efforts to pull clear, the hefty old steam wagon collided with the Morris, flattening two wheels and precipitating father through the windscreen. He was saved from serious injury by that bastion of British dignity, his bowler hat and the party scrambled out, shaken but not seriously hurt.

By a happy chance, the vehicle behind was a lorry owned by a brewery and the driver, a man of obvious initiative and resource who recognised an emergency when he saw one, foraged among his stock for medicinal sustenance. The whole party then sat by the roadside taking refreshment while the mess was sorted out. The Morris Oxford was subsequently replaced by a 15 cwt. motor van.

The year 1927 was a milestone in Lindseys career, for they applied for, and were granted, membership of the National Association of Master Heating and Domestic Engineers (later to become the Heating and Ventilating Contractors Association). The early 1930s was the era of the great depression and in common with others, the business had a lean time. But the loyal support and efforts of the staff enabled the firm to survive.

Charles Junior recalled a touching episode that illustrates the loyalty and character of the staff Lindseys have always been fortunate to possess. Lack of work had forced them, as a last resort, to lay off one of their fitters. But the next day came an enquiry from Leytonstone some 40 miles away.

As Charles said: 'In those days you went after everything and you went after it quick!'. The out-of-work fitter, who happened to be in the yard when the news came, immediately volunteered to go along and help "And he did it without any expectation of payment or reward".

But as business gathered momentum, the training programme of the early years bore fruit and an organised staff of highly skilled and competent engineers and craftsmen was available to meet it. The firm was given contracts for the installation of many heating and ventilating systems in schools, factories and country houses throughout Essex. A new breakthrough in the 1930s were contracts for the design and installation of heating and ventilating systems in a large number of ships, experience which was to pay dividends during and after the war years.

With the call from architects and other professional bodies, along with private contracts for the design of increasingly complex and efficient types of systems, expansion became a necessity and in 1936 new and larger premises, designed to meet the special needs of the industry, were built in Maldon Road. Now, too, the business was incorporated as a limited company: C H Lindsey and Son Ltd.

To celebrate the occasion, the company decided to acquire a motif connected in some way both with the activities of the business, and with Colchester, its home town. Mindful of the town's Roman traditions and of the fame of the Romans

Top: *The workforce in the 1960s.*

as heating engineers, Charles junior spent much time in discussions with the Curator of Colchester Museum. Their deliberations and researches unearthed an illustration of a three-legged brazier which was used by the Romans for heating and warming purposes. A stylised version was adapted as the firm's symbol and appears to this day on the company's letter-headings and publicity.

The year 1939 came and with it, another war. C H Lindsey and Son Ltd switched all their energies to the war effort, installing heating and ventilation in Royal Air Force stations, military camps, hospitals and munitions factories. In addition a considerable part of the firm's output was turned to engineering services on minesweepers and other naval craft built in the shipyards at Wivenhoe and Rowhedge, the experience gained in the mid-1930s paying off and ensuring that once again Lindseys were where action was, and fully prepared. And not only to assist in building the ships - some of the staff volunteered as part of the crews that delivered them from the builders' yards to such ports as Dover, Portsmouth, Plymouth, Immingham and Hull. This motley gathering of 'land-lubbers' had some rare adventures and Charles Junior said that in his time he did every job on a ship from deck-hand to chief engineer.

One never-to-be-forgotten encounter, in the middle of the Thames, was with swarms of rabbits! It seems that the seafaring bunnies were bred on board by the men manning the block ships moored in the river, and sold on the meat-starved mainland! An astonishing sight, though after a drink or two!

Peace in 1945 and Lindseys like everyone else, had to shake off the problems of war and rebuild life on a peacetime footing. Shortages of materials and the general upheaval of war made this a tricky period, but the spirit of enterprise and comradeship which had always been a feature of Lindseys paid off, the difficulties were overcome and the aims and ambitions for the further growth and success of the firm were resumed.

In the 1950s the third generation of Lindseys came into the business with the arrival on the scene of Charles G Lindsey and Richard, sons of Charles R Lindsey. Both attended the National College in London obtaining the Diploma for Heating, Ventilating and Air Conditioning and were admitted to Corporate membership of the Institution of Heating and Ventilating Engineers.

January 1952 brought a sad event with the death of 'The Governor', Charles Hepburn Lindsey, at the age of eighty. The firm he started on a hand-cart had taken massive strides into the electronic age and his closing years had been full of the satisfaction of seeing his son and grandsons thriving in the business and continuing the first-class standards of workmanship and service to the clients upon which he had always insisted. Over the years this policy had borne fruit and made the name Lindsey a by-word for craftsmanship and reliability.

With the onset of the 1960s, expansion continued and the Company moved to new and larger premises at 78 East Hill, Colchester. With the advent of the electronic age, high standards of temperature, humidity control, automatic firing, air conditioning and unobtrusive systems became not merely desirable, but essential. Natural gas made its debut and the heating and ventilating business boomed for those who were prepared for the almost daily developments in personal comfort and increasing sophistication.

Below: *1960s workers with one of the company's vehicles.*

To meet these needs, Lindseys introduced new and revised methods in the drawing office and on site. Turnover rose accordingly, and in co-operation with many well-known architects and with recommendations from previous customers, Lindseys obtained orders and repeat orders for heating, ventilating and air conditioning systems both locally and in many parts of England. One contract even took them to Spain, where the firm installed a sophisticated system to enable a horticulturist to grow orchids in an area which had perfect daytime temperatures but very cold night winds.

The 1970s brought an awareness for fuel conservation and with it the need for more energy saving devices to be incorporated within system designs. It was also essential for existing installations to receive regular routine maintenance visits in order to keep them in pristine condition and maintain optimum efficiency. Lindseys recognised this need and formed a special department to carry out regular maintenance to a whole range of domestic and commercial systems.

In 1975 the Company, by now numbering nearly 100 employees celebrated its Golden Jubilee with a grand dinner/dance at the George Hotel in Colchester High Street. At that time 'The George' still had the Vanderville Ballroom which made a splendid venue for such a gathering. By this time a number of employees had been with the Company approaching 50 years and several gold watches were presented that night.

Expansion continued through into the 1980s with Charles G and Richard at the helm. Come 1984, Charles R who, with his father had founded the Company nearly 60 years before, died at the age of 80.

During this period the fourth generation of the Lindsey family, in the shape of Charles D and Robert, sons of Charles G joined the Company together with Richard Pearce, grandson of Charles R. Charles D studied at Loughborough University and gained a degree in Environmental Engineering whilst Robert, following university, concentrated his efforts on setting up departments to specialise in the design and maintenance of the new high-tech air conditioning systems, soon to become a major part of many commercial buildings. The 1980s was also a time when loyal employees who had served Lindseys for the whole of their working life began to retire.

By 1990, again continued expansion meant that the East Hill premises were too small and business was being

Below: *The early 1980s workforce.*
Bottom: *Apprentices receiving tuition from a senior craftsman.*

were maintained with the arrival on the staff of Christopher Lindsey son of Richard.

During recent years Lindseys emphasis has very much turned towards air conditioning and, as we pass into the next Millennium, they are in excellent shape to move forward to their 75th anniversary.

Whatever developments the future may bring in heating ventilating or air conditioning, Lindseys will be right there, even as the two men with their hand card were in 1925 with their magical array of pipes, boilers, pumps and hot water cylinders which brought a hitherto undreamed of dimension in warmth and comfort to improve the quality of life.

Above left: A typical Lindsey installation.
Top: Today's office building and maintenance fleet.
Below: Part of today's design office.

somewhat curtailed because of traffic congestion near to the town centre. So, Charles G and Richard looked for a new location where expansion could continue and easy access to main routes was possible. The ideal solution came from Colchester Borough Council, who were at that time selling land at Severalls Lane for business premises. A plot was bought in Brunel Way and a purpose designed building erected, large enough to cope with expansion well into the next millennium. A commemorative stone was laid in the new building by Bill Abbott and Les Bloomfield, two long since retired members of staff who had each worked 50 years for the Company.

Established in the new premises business prospered even throughout the recession that blighted the early 90s. A sad occurrence in 1994 was the accidental death of Robert Lindsey, by then a director of the company. He is greatly missed even to this day. But the level of family connections

TJ Evers Ltd- building the future

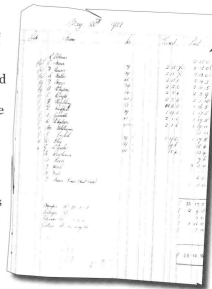

TJ Evers Ltd, named after the founder of the firm - Thomas James - a carpenter who established the business towards the end of the first world war, has been responsible for the construction of many prestigious modern buildings. But before we examine the impressive client and project lists which the company has built up, it would be interesting to return briefly to the days of T J Evers himself and his first two assistants (and a wheelbarrow!) to look at the foundations of what has become a well-established, well-respected family firm. Just back from the Great War, Thomas James Evers knew from the start the kind of firm he intended to build - no fly-by-night cowboy operation this. From the start, Tom Evers believed in quality, professionalism and traditional craftsmanship, happy to earn only a few pounds a week, pushing his barrow, whilst building a reputation which would be the company's best advertisement. Growing numbers of satisfied customers enabled the company to increase its staff and consequently its level of expertise and experience. In 1943 T J Evers became a limited company.

Those original beliefs of Tom's still steer the company today. However, as one member of staff has been known to declare, 'You cannot survive - let alone thrive and prosper - in the construction industry for 80 years on tradition alone'. Indeed, to survive for over 80 years in the construction

industry is astonishing and only the excellent quality of TJ Evers' work, together with sound managerial practices, has made it possible.

Still very much a family firm - the business being passed down to his son, Alan, with his son Michael later becoming chairman - the firm has built its way up from those two assistants and a few pounds a week income, to a staff of over a hundred, and a yearly turnover of over eight million pounds. The fourth generation of the family is now firmly ensconced with the founder's great grandson joining the company.

So, let's look at what's so special about this particular construction company. With a client list including such names as the BBC, Marconi, Royal Mail, Asda Stores, Barclays Bank and Prudential Assurance, to name only a

Above left: *Tom Evers, founder.*
Above right: *A page from a wages book dating from 1932.*
Below: *One of the trucks used in the 1950s.*

small number of the many high-profile companies seeking their help, it's obvious they're doing something right! Many local authorities and government organisations, including Colchester Borough Council, Essex County Council, Ipswich Borough Council and the Property Services Agency, have called on their expertise. The list of major projects completed is equally impressive. One of the earlier projects completed was the Maldon Grammar school, but today the list includes banks, hotels, hospitals, restaurants and municipal buildings and Colchester's Mercury Theatre (the original building as well as the more recent extensions). Not content with the construction of a variety of new buildings, TJ Evers Ltd has also been responsible for the restoration of many old East Anglian buildings - including a sensitive and well-received conversion of the Grade II listed barn at Maldon Hall Farm into a residential property - and complementary extensions to existing structures. One of the most highly-praised projects was the £3.4 million contract to

build the student accommodation for Essex University in Colchester.

TJ Evers Ltd have for many years been involved in providing local housing for Colne Housing Society. Other contracts include The Dutch Quarter,

the redevelopment of Balkerne Gardens, Colchester Barracks, Parsley House, The Post Office and Colchester Institute (formerly North East Essex Technical College) where they have completed many projects since 1972.

Probably the one constant thread running through the history and tradition of T J Evers' work is quality. The company is keen to upgrade the reputation of the construction industry and not to be associated with those builders who cut and run when problems arise. Evers staff are well aware of the generally poor image of builders - the falling-down jeans and the wolf-whistling jack-the-lads - and work to enhance the industry's reputation through their own high-quality work. Michael Evers, long associated with the firm in a managerial capacity, indicates the difference in dealing with a company, like themselves, committed to quality. 'Things will go wrong sometimes. It's how the contractor deals with the problems that's important. We don't walk away, we deal with it. That's the difference between us and the cowboy element.'

Over eighty years after its founding the company is organised on a more formal basis, with different departments covering different aspects of the work. One such department is the Small Contracts Department, which was set up in 1970 to meet the needs of those with smaller, more specialised building requirements. These could include restorations and small building projects.

Another separate area is Tiptree Joinery Services, which handles the highly-skilled joinery work demanded by

Above centre: *An early letterhead.* ***Top:*** *Stanway School built 1956/57.* ***Left:*** *Balkerne Gardens.*

corporate clients and restorations. Skilled craftspeople work in both hardwood and softwood to produce high quality items for both Evers' projects and general buyers. The fact that several major clients and building contractors have come back to Evers for repeat projects speaks well of the loyalty their standard of work engenders.

Whilst TJ Evers' reputation for quality of work is foremost, another important aspect of the company is the management skills they have developed over the years. This takes the shape not only of computerisation, but in offering a full package of services - cost analysis, estimating and surveying - the aim being to complete projects to budget and on time.

The management expertise is again highlighted in the loyalty of many staff - staff are treated well to encourage them to stay with the firm, and this certainly seems to have been successful so far, with staff turnover much lower than

in the industry generally. The joinery shop staff in particular seem happy in their work - over 75 per cent of them have been with the company for a number of years. One joinery employee, Denis Baker, was presented at the company's 80th birthday celebrations in 1998, with a gold watch to mark his own 40 years of service, which started when he left school.

In order to continue to offer clients the level of expertise they require the company feels it is vital to not only recruit the right people and look after them well, but also to set training for current, and also possibly future employees, high on the agenda.

TJ Evers is a forward-looking company, keeping ahead in a competitive industry, and its commitment to training indicates how seriously it takes its responsibility for the future of construction work generally. Together with other companies of a similar size, TJ Evers played a key role in setting up the

Above: *Highwoods Primary School, Colchester.*
Top: *Essex University student accomodation, built by the company.* **Left:** *The specialist joinery service.*

abreast of current construction methods in order to offer an ever-higher standard of work more efficiently. Close relations with a number of architects facilitates progress in this direction. Their aim is to build more attractive and comfortable buildings, using modern materials without harming the environment. Certainly a worthy mission for these environmentally-aware times.

Over the years the company has built up a reputation within its industry, accepting awards such as the Southend-on-Sea Borough Council Design Awards Commendation for Thorpe Infants School; Kent Blaxhill and Building Employers Confederation Merit Award for good work to a restricted specification; Colchester Borough Council Access Award; Highly Commended Housing Award from the Secretary of State for the Environment; Kent Blaxhill and Building Employers Confederation Merit Award for Brickwork and Kent Blaxhill and Building Employers Confederation Merit Award for Joinery and Finishes.

Whilst the company headquarters is in the same place in Tiptree as it was when it was founded all those years ago, it's doubtful that Tom Evers would recognise it. The wheelbarrow's long gone and the workforce has increased somewhat, but one thing he would certainly recognise and be proud of, is the level of craftsmanship which, throughout the years, has remained constant. He would be delighted that the reputation he nurtured as a young man is still as impressive as it was in the early days, and that his fledgling company, offering work to just three people, has remained a well-regarded family firm, offering employment to over one hundred well-trained and committed staff.

Essex Construction Training Group to put on courses and build up links with schools, emphasising the many facets of building work to youngsters considering their futures. Many do not realise the many careers within construction and the level of ability required for most of them. TJ Evers wishes to play a full part in bringing this to their attention in the hope that a skills shortage can be avoided.

Training is just one aspect of Evers' sound long-term strategy to update the construction industry in general, and their own company in particular, with the new millennium. They have also firmly grasped the equal opportunities nettle by employing at least one woman in the joinery shop, believing that the construction industry should be sold to young people of both sexes as a career opportunity. And environmental concerns, much to the forefront at present, are taken equally seriously, the company stating that they recognise their 'environmental responsibility in energy conservation' and their 'duty to preserve and protect our surroundings and the conservation of natural resources'. In a company dealing with the restoration of many old buildings, this is reassuring for clients, locals and environmentalists alike.

So the firm has the future sewn up? Well, if so, they're in no danger of becoming complacent! Keen not to be seen as trading on past successes alone, TJ Evers believe in keeping

Above: *The extension to Wickham Bishops Church.* ***Top:*** *The extension to the Mercury Theatre. The company built the original theatre as well as the recent extensions.* ***Below:*** *One of the company's employees at work.*

Moving the earth to satisfy the customer

We often think of the 50s and 60s as the period when Britain's motorway network grew. Of course, motorways do not simply grow - they have to be built; and so during this period a number of companies with the requisite skills and expertise began to thrive.

One such company was Blackwell. The founder, Chris Blackwell, began his contracting career at the end of the second world war, undertaking local agricultural contracts and progressing to larger machinery which enabled him to take on earth-moving work on a grander scale. Between 1946-56 contracts included earthworks for an oil refinery at Southampton, a reservoir at Northampton, the Marks Tey racecourse, and work on Canvey Island following the 1953 floods. In 1956 Chris formed his own company, together with his brother Dick and workmates Harry Ayton, Bill Smith, Doug Heard, Ronnie Ratcliffe, Aubrey Botting, Neville Davery, Ken Boyer, Tom Bowyer, 'Wag' Waghorn - and others. The first major contract to which the new company put its name was a stretch of earthworks on the first section of the M1. Blackwell put nine DW21 motor scrapers onto the job - thus sharing in a piece of civil engineering history, as this was the first time that motor scrapers were used on a civil engineering project in this country.

Blackwell's M1 contract was followed by work on the M2 in Kent; and from here the firm went on to its first big rock job, on the Clevedon Hills section of the M5, which at £2.3 million represented its largest ever contract at that time. By the end of 1978 Blackwell had designed, built and moved into in its prestigious new Head Office at Earls Colne. In little more than two decades the company had grown into an efficient, reliable and highly-respected major contractor, with an experienced and loyal staff and an impressive plant holding of earthmoving equipment. Particularly appreciated was its ability to adapt its working practices to cope with unforeseen circumstances so as to ensure high quality workmanship and timely completion, even when faced with the unexpected.

The 1980s brought ambitious plans for the construction of a circular motorway around London, and Blackwell took several contracts including that for the Brentwood section of the M25. Plant deployed on this job included a 460 hp Caterpillar D9L bulldozer; costing £257,900 and delivered to Blackwells on the day it celebrated its 25th anniversary, this

Above left: *Chris Blackwell, founder of the company.* ***Below:*** *A picture dating from c1950.* ***Bottom:*** *Work on the M1 motorway in the late 1950s. Blackwell had nine scrapers working on the project - this proved to be a turning point for the company.*

remembered with the greatest of affection and respect by all who worked alongside him and was also well known in the racing world, having bred a number of successful racehorses. A man of many interests, he might be remembered by readers who used to listen to Radio 390 during the 60s for his support of the station when it became a target of the Government's campaign to eliminate pirate radio.

The family involvement in the managment of the company finally came to an end in 1993 when Chris' brother Dick retired as Managing Director after 37 years. However, two of Chris' grandchildren, Caroline and Ben, have since started their careers with Blackwell. The family connection therefore continues, as does the firm's success. Over the last decade or so Blackwell become increasingly involved in infrastructure and groundworks, landfill sites, sewerage and sewage treatment, culverts and drainage, earth retention, road upgrades and improvements and motorway maintenance. The founder's policy of investing in equipment to expand the potential of the firm continues to pay dividends: equipment for installing band drains, acquired at the beginning of the 90s, led to development of the Geotechnics division. Skills acquired over the years also enable the company to provide engineering services to outside plant operators, servicing, maintaining, overhauling and rebuilding earthmoving plant, and in fact its Engineering Services division won the prestigious Castolin Eutectic Conservationist of the Year Award. Expertise in all aspects of land regeneration is also offered. Safety and environmental issues are taken very seriously, with the company committed to fulfilling all responsibilities, whether towards employees, clients or the environment. As principal contractor, Blackwell observes strict quality assurance procedures coupled with effective time and resource management to ensure successful and timely completion in full compliance with the contract. From the very beginning, the company has founded its reputation on the quality of its performance, and this fundamental principle remains unaltered. Chris Blackwell would be proud to know that, throughout the construction industry and beyond, his name is still associated with success and quality.

was the first of its kind in Britain and only the second in the whole of Europe, and was the most powerful machine the firm had ever owned.

Other major highways contracts around that time included the Colchester Eastern Coggeshall and Braintree By-Passes; in due course, however, the country's road-building programme was wound down. Blackwell transferred its skills and expertise to a wider variety of projects, and also extended its operations into other geographical locations. Its first subsidiary company had been set up in Northern Ireland during the 1960s when Blackwell was working on the Ballymena Bypass; further Northern Ireland contracts followed and this office continued to operate until 1981. In 1987 the Swansea office was established to handle contracts in South Wales. A recent contract carried out in Clwyd consisted of rock buttressing to a small lane near Bettws Gwerfil Goch, and the intriguing thing about this job was what had made it necessary. It seems that sheep had a habit of trying to find shelter from the elements in the side of an embankment, and over the years their feet scrape out so much material that the road is undermined!

The firm suffered a sad blow when its founder and Chairman, Chris Blackwell, died suddenly in 1990. Chris is

Above: *The company premises at Earls Colne.*
Top: *Workers in the 1970s.*
Right: *The arrival of the company's first Cat. D9L tractor - the first of its kind.*

Staying afloat after 130 years

The 25th February 1870 was the founding moment of J J Prior Limited and the beginning of what was to become a Prior family business passed down through the generations, that is still thriving today, well over a century later.

James John Prior, the founding member of the transport company, was born in Great Samford, Essex in 1844 and spent the first 16 years of his life as a farm labourer. Over the following 10 years however, his ambition led him to London where he worked for several companies earning enough money to enable him to buy a few horses and to lease premises and so establishing J J Prior Ltd.

James worked hard to build his new business. Only 18 years after J J Prior Ltd was founded, a lease with the Great Eastern Railway was signed for Orchard Wharf which became the companies new premises. In 1918, nine months after James' death his grandson A J C Prior, or Mr Bert as he was affectionately known to his employees, joined the company making it a family business. By this time, J J Prior owned three farms, about two hundred horses and carts, steam rollers, three sailing barges, three lorries and premises in Loughton, Bermondsey and Poplar. With the help of his brothers James and Len, who joined him in 1928, Bert began expanding the business.

He gradually acquired a fleet of motor barges, mainly transporting sand and gravel. This new arm of the business led to the purchasing of a sand marketing company at Fingringhoe in 1934 and subsequently, the forming of J J Prior (Aggregates) Ltd.

The war years brought with them a diversion for J J Prior Ltd. The fleet of Prior's barges were used in the war effort and even helped with the evacuation of troops from Dunkirk. A surviving report from the master of the Sherfield barge dated 1st June 1940 describes the harrowing journey to Dunkirk, 'On arrival at Dunkirk we were bombed and machine-gunned by German planes, causing severe shaking to our boat. Our red Ensign was shot away by gunfire, wheelhouse windows smashed , also glasses in the skylight cracked...".

Above left: *James John Prior, founder of the company.*
Below: *The 'Bert Prior' in rough seas.*
Bottom: *The River Colne at Fingringhoe in the 1930s.*

In 1947, after the war years, Berts' son Peter joined the business and on the death of his father in 1976, he became the Chairman as well as the Managing Director of J J Prior Transport Ltd. By this time J J Prior Ltd now owned Orchard Wharf and the adjacent Silvocea Wharf. The family business was now involved in road and river transport, barge and tug building, production and distribution of sand and gravel and the repair and maintenance of barges, lorries, cranes and other machinery.

Despite the loss of several of their premises in Limehouse, Stepney and Bermondsey in the 1950s due to a scourge of compulsory purchases, J J Prior Ltd continued to survive as a family business. Len Prior's son, Colin joined the business in 1952 and became a director in 1957, also the freehold of Brewery Wharf in Greenwich was purchased during this decade. The advent of the 1960s saw two new barges built for the Prior fleet, one of which was named the 'Bert Prior" after the founders grandson. Bert's grandson, Mark Prior joined the family business in 1971 and helped J J Prior Ltd to survive through the recessions of the early 70s and

80s. In 1984 Mark became Managing Director of the company and in the same year added yet another barge to the growing Prior fleet.

Despite being able to overcome past set-backs the late 80s marked a period of difficulty that would prove impossible to conquer. On 6th January 1986, the London Docklands Development Corporation published its Leamouth Area Draft Development Plan which unfortunately, signified the beginning of the end for the Prior East London home. Despite a valiant effort to save Orchard and Silvocea Wharves by the Priors they were compulsorily acquired by the London Docklands Development Corporation on 29th June 1990 and the Priors relocated their headquarters back to Fingringhoe in Essex.

This misfortune however, was short lived. The1990s was a time of celebration for the Priors. 1994 marked 60 years in the sand and gravel industry and in1995 the family celebrated the 125th anniversary of the foundation of the company. In 1997 and1998 the business was judged one of the top quarry operators in Essex. A larger vessel, the Holm Sound, able to carry 600 tonnes of material, was also purchased in 1998 after being renamed 'Peter Prior' in a ceremony performed by Glenda Jackson MP.

J J Prior Transport Ltd, with its environmentally friendly methods of transport, plans to stay afloat for at least another 130 years, continuing to develop and grow whilst maintaining its family tradition and local connections.

Above left: *The 'Peter Prior' joins the fleet.*
Top: *Ballast Quay in the 1960s.*

A *driving force in Colchester*

D C Osborne Ltd has come a long way over the past four decades since it was established in 1958. The local company began life when Denis Osborne opened a small bicycle shop in Colchester. In doing so, Denis became the founder of D C Osborne Ltd as it continues to be known today, but trading as Osborne Garages. Denis soon added to his range of products and undertook the first of many expansions to come by starting to sell mopeds. Eventually, only four years after establishing his business, Denis became one of the earliest dealers in the UK to take on the Honda agency and the bicycle shop became a Honda motorcycle dealership.

The mid to late 60s saw the growth of the company and yet another four years after becoming a Honda dealer Denis instigated another expansion for Osborne Garages. This time, further progress meant moving premises and leaving the bicycle shop behind. The new and improved premises for the company were situated at North Station Road. This move marked a significant transition for the business which was to shape the direction of the future of Osborne Garages as a Honda car dealer. This expansion meant that in 1972 the motorcycle sales section of the business had to be moved to Colchester's East Hill.

In 1978, twenty years after Osborne Garages was founded, the site at North Station Road was redeveloped creating one of the first purpose built Honda showrooms dedicated solely to selling Honda cars. However, two years later in 1980, not content with standing still, Osborne Garages took another step forward and procured a Mitsubishi franchise.

Denis Osborne's son, Paul, like his father began his career by setting up his own company. At the age of eighteen Paul was selling motorcycles, spares and accessories. He built up his own business and acquired two franchises, including one for Honda motorcycles, and successfully ran two shops. In 1981 however, he sold his business in order to join the family firm working for his father as Sales Director. By 1985, Denis had handed the principal management of the business over to Paul who succeeded his father as Managing Director of Osborne Garages. Paul immediately set to work implementing a five year development plan concentrating on overall growth of the organisation and the upgrading of staff and services within it.

1988, the 30th anniversary year of the company, marked the next big step for Osborne Garages when they invested

Above: *Early advertising.* ***Below:*** *Denis Osborne at the door of the motorcycle dealership circa 1964.*

over £1 million in a new Honda showroom and garage. The new garage, whose showroom alone covers some 6300 square feet, was constructed on a 'green field' site and was designed to reflect the Honda corporate image.

1990 was marked with both good and bad fortune for Osborne Garages. Sadly, Denis Osborne died in this year. However, continuing in the tradition of constant expansion and growth that Denis himself had initiated, the company also acquired Honda Chelmsford from Lancaster Garages. Two years later in 1992, Osborne Garages branched out once again when they acquired Neep of Colchester, a BMW showroom and workshop. This purchase was consolidated when another BMW garage, Neep of London was acquired in 1996 from LJK Garages.

Osborne Garages developed a brand new Mitsubishi Centre in Colchester in 1999 adding further to their assets. This new centre in Ipswich Road, with a showroom of 4000 square feet and 60 prime forecourt spaces boasts, 'the most advanced state of the art facilities, ahead of any other UK Mitsubishi dealership'.

The rapid growth of Osborne Garages since its establishment in 1958, has transformed it from a family run business where everybody knew each other and everything that was going on, to a still growing company with nearly 200 employees throughout the six centres, working in partnership with five manufacturers. Despite this, the company still works hard to value their employees and indeed, has embarked upon the Investors In People programme. The company also produces a news letter, 'Inside Line' three times a year to keep everybody informed about their colleagues and the company's progress. The sponsorship of one of Essex's largest cricket leagues along with the local rugby team also ensures that the company retains its ties with the local community.

Osborne Garages will maintain its history of expansion and growth as the development and acquisition of further dealerships is planned for the future.

Above left: *The North Station Road garage before redevelopment in 1978...*
Top: *...and after.*
Below: *The Honda dealership at Ipswich Road today.*

Pressing ahead - MGE

It was in 1945 that MGE commenced business as an installer of all types of electrical equipment. Mr. S A Martin was the founder of the company that was originally set up under the name of M G Electric (Colchester) Limited. Five years after the establishment of M G Electric (Colchester) Limited, the business had begun to flourish and was already in position to expand. In the early 1950s a small factory was built to start production of fractional horse-power electric motors. These motors proved to be a success and over the next few years the company gained a good reputation for the manufacture of high quality, reliable electric motors, supplying regular customers in the fan industry as well as several British government ministries. Indeed, at this time the company was one of only two British companies accepted to supply electric fan motors for use in military equipment! Another widely known client was the original Rank Xerox

Above: The company's founder, Mr S A Martin.
Below: The firm's premises in the 1950s.

copier production in Britain. In 1954 the company seized the opportunity to branch out from producing only electric motors. A client company manufacturing and selling surgical suction equipment had got into financial difficulties and gone into liquidation. Subsequently, M G Electric acquired the business and embarked on a process of enhancing and improving the range of products. Indeed, this branch of the business forms a sizeable proportion of the company as a whole today.

It was realised that if the company wished to grow in a more positive and controlled manner, it was essential that it produce its own products. With this policy in mind, a range of electric coolant pumps for use in the machine tool industry was designed. M G Electric became a major supplier of the equipment to the British market and prior to the 1970s was the sole supplier of coolant pumps to companies such as Colchester Lathe Company, Alfred Herbert, Adcock and Shipley, Jones and Shipman and Myford. At this time the company were carrying out most of their own engineering, involving machining, die casting, tool making, sheet metal fabrication and electric motor winding. However, all except the electric motor winding were gradually phased out.

The 1970s marked a difficult period in the domestic machine tool industry and eventually its demise! With considerable foresight, the company made a conscious effort to diversify. The production of a range of dampening and circulation equipment, sold to British print manufacturers, was initiated and the product range was widened when an agreement was signed with Royse US. This agreement allowed M G Electric to manufacture and sell Royse dampening

equipment throughout Europe, Australia, Singapore and Hong Kong. The agreement also advantageously gave the company access to the Alcomiser, a patented alcohol control device used in the dampening and circulation unit today.

This arrangement with Royce continued for 15 years, during which time M G Electric developed the product further until, finally, it parted company from Royce and began to promote the product as its own. At about the same time, in 1985, the company moved from Whitehall Industrial Estate to Wyncolls road.

The early 1990s were years of recession and the growth of the company was accordingly affected. However, it was during this time that the company was awarded a British Standard Quality accreditation and in 1995 celebrated its 50th year in business. The continued success of the company enabled them to move their engineers into purpose-built premises in Colchester and invest £150,000 refurbishing a 10,000 sq ft industrial unit close to the existing site in Wyncolls road, thus expanding their research and development facilities.

Throughout its history M G Electric has remained within the hands of the founder's family with the current chairman being the founder's son, Mr. Michael Martin. In 1998 Graham Martin, grandson of the founder, became the Managing Director of M G Electric. In 1999 MGE, as the company is now known, created a new image for itself in the current global marketplace with its new company logo - MGE Worldwide - and the launch of its company website. This comes on top of a two-year training period undergone as part of a £1.3 million European Union funding scheme, which has enabled the

> *In 1954 the company seized the opportunity to branch out from producing only electric motors*

company to expand its production operation. Today, MGE is a leading manufacturer in the field of printing press temperature control and medical suction equipment. 75 per cent of the products manufactured are exported to countries as far afield as Japan, Brazil and Australia as well as to our closer European neighbours. However, in spite of the extensive global opportunities pursued by the company, it remains a medium-sized family firm continuing to provide employment for the local population and business for other locally based companies from which it sources the majority of its components. MGE and the founder's family have been a part of Colchester life for the past 50 years and intend to remain so well into the future.

Bottom: *The premises ready to take on the new millennium.*

Building on the success of previous generations

ven as a little boy, the founder Robert George Carter knew what he wanted to be when he grew up - he wanted to be a carpenter, like his grandfather. And this was the first of many wise decisions which have led to the R G Carter Group becoming the successful, well-respected construction company that it is today.

Young George, as he chose to be called (George was his grandfather's name) became a carpenter's apprentice at the age of 14, practising his new skills with the tools he had inherited from his grandfather. After his apprenticeship he tried life in London, decided it was not for him, and returned to East Anglia, where he spent the next few years working alongside experienced craftsmen who displayed the high level of skill that was to become so important to George.

In 1914 George Carter joined up and served in France. His bravery, which almost cost him his life on a number of occasions, earned him the Military Medal and the Croix de Guerre. Within three days of being demobbed he found employment on a building site in Norwich; he quickly rose to foreman and then to general foreman, and by 1921 he was married and rnnning his own business.

Below: *The dilapidated farmhouse at Highwoods that was to become the Rovers Tye public house.*
Right: *The Rovers Tye public house.*

From the outset, the whole family was involved in the venture; his uncles helped him financially, his wife Florence acted as secretary, bookkeeper and wages clerk and her brother Ted drove the horse and trolley, and later the motor lorry. George worked tirelessly to get his business up and running, but always managed to find time for his children, Robert Edward, Betty, Mary and Ruth. Where work was concerned, his guiding rule was that a contract had to be completed on time even if it meant working from six in the morning until ten in the evening during the summer months. When a contract was finished he liked to put up hoardings emblazoned with the firm's proud boast, On Time Again! He would not tolerate timewasters,

Those early landmark buildings set the seal on a rapid rise in the fortunes of R G Carter Colchester. It soon needed a bigger and more permanent base, and by 1976 had moved to its present site at 5 Grange Way, on the Whitehall Industrial Estate (Telephone 01206 794455).

Since then the company, which now employs 130 people, has continued to play a major part in shaping the face of the garrison town.

Among its notable landmarks is the former dilapidated farmhouse that is now the Rovers Tye public house at Highwoods, which opened in the mid-1980s. Also in the public eye was the conversion of the old Hyams clothing factory into offices now occupied by Stanley Bragg Architects, and the SGR FM radio station.

but he would reward hard work, and this created great loyalty among his workforce.

Having survived the depression of the late 1920s and early 1930s, George decided in 1932 to turn the firm into a limited company. His son Bob joined R G Carter Limited as an apprentice carpenter six years later, but unfortunately his early career was interrupted, as his father's had been, by the outbreak of war. The firm obtained a steady stream of Government contracts; one of the more unusual jobs the construction of a fake city, complete with homes and factories, at Withernsea, as a decoy to draw German bombers away from nearby Hull.

Bob Carter returned in 1946, and took over as managing director in 1950. In the early 50s, under Bob Carter's leadership, business began to boom, and by the mid-1950s, R G Carter had become the largest building firm in Norfolk.

A small office in Culver Street marked R G Carter's modest start in Colchester in 1973. Its first contract was to construct Wellington House, an office block in Butt Road, the success of which soon led to the building of a major office complex next to Colchester North Station for electrical giant Phillips.

More recently, in 1997, the company carried out another public service contract for the town, creating the scenic lift and staircase that links the Vineyard Street market and car park with the Red Lion shopping precinct.

Other notables are the police station in Southway, built in 1988; the Royal London insurance building at Middleborough (1993); and the NCP multi-storey car park in Osborne Street (1991).

The Group is currently enjoying the most successful period in its history under the chairmanship of Robert Carter, Bob's son. This family tradition, now in its third generation, is a crucial element in the stability and security of the workforce and the continued expansion and success of the company.

Above left: *The NCP multi-storey car park on Osborne Street.* ***Top:*** *The office block originally built for the Phillips Corporation.*

The company with a piping hot future

The year 2000 marks the 30th anniversary of Essex Heating Supplies Ltd. Although compared with many local companies it is still in its infancy, Essex Heating Supplies has already achieved a level of success which many might envy. Since March 1970, the month in which it first came into existence, the company has built up a reputation both for the quality of its service and for the wide range of products which it keeps in stock - hence its proud claim to be, in all circumstances, 'the professionals' choice'.

Essex Heating Supplies was set up at 50 Military Road, Colchester, for the distribution of heating and plumbing materials, by partners Peter Manby, Geoff Eldred and Ray Embling. All three partners already had a good grounding in the trade, having gained their experience by working for other merchants before setting up their own company. Experience, in a specialised trade such as this, is perhaps the most valuable asset, and so the new venture prospered. After two years the business moved to premises in Chandlers Row, on the Port Lane Trading Estate. Ray stayed with the company for only a couple of years, Geoff retiring some years later, which left Peter Manby as the only one of the original founders still with the business. But despite the changes in personnel, the firm's success continued. It is possible, of course, that the recognisable blue liveried lorries with the stylish logo and name painted on the side in bright yellow,

a familiar sight on the roads of East Anglia, may have helped to spread the word; used for deliveries, the lorries fulfilled a useful secondary role as a travelling advertisement, promoting the company as a useful source of supply for 'plumbing-heating-bathrooms'. Essex Heating has always recognised the importance of letting people know it is there - readers may remember its recent radio advertising campaign through SGR - and this was particularly important when the oil crisis hit Britain in the 70s, and industry struggled to keep going on a three-day week. These were difficult times even for established firms, and the fledgling companies of the time had to battle against all odds. Many went to the wall, but Essex Heating Supplies Ltd survived, thanks to a combination of hard work, experience, a growing reputation and good management. Since then these same qualities have pulled the firm through three recessions - which, as the company is only too well aware, always hit the building trade first.

Above: An early brochure advertising the company's products. *Below (both pictures):* The sales counter in the 1970s.

manufacturers' latest bathroom suites, shower units and accessories.

Deservedly, Essex Heating Supplies is held in high regard by professional plumbing and heating contractors, both small and large, as well as its other main clients, the local authorities and housing associations. Servicing both the domestic and the commercial market, Essex Heating Supplies can supply virtually any items that a plumbing and heating engineer is likely to need, from a combi boiler to a set of gold bath taps. Whether installing a new heating system or bathroom, upgrading an existing system or carrying out repairs, customers know that EHS offers best value for money products and can provide expert advice to assist in selecting an item whose performance matches their requirements. In addition to everything needed to heat a home and furnish a bathroom, the firm also stocks a full range of drainage products including guttering and waste pipes.

In just 30 years Essex Heating has grown from its beginnings as a small, privately-owned concern to a company with a turnover of £38 million a year and a stock-holding of £5 million. It has spread far beyond its native Essex to service London, Kent and the whole of East Anglia from one centre in Colchester. Customers can trade with the company at any one of its extensive network of branches. In Essex, outlets are situated at Braintree, Chelmsford, Harlow, Ilford, Romford and

The one piece of good fortune for the company in the midst of the general climate of gloom which prevailed during the 70s was the continuing nationwide boom in central heating. This had begun at the end of the previous decade, largely as a result of the imposition of smokeless zones throughout the country which compelled many households to look for an alternative to their old coal fires. However, as the advantages of central heating became more widely known, it caught on in a big way, until the vast majority of homes had invested in having a central heating system installed. Before long central heating had become a standard expectation of homebuyers and virtually all new houses were built with central heating included as part of the original specification - which, of course, was good news for Essex Heating Supplies.

By 1988 Essex Heating's Head Office had moved to Wyncolls Road, on the Severalls Industrial Park. The company still operates from both Port Lane and Wyncolls Road, with a sales counter at both premises, and a bathroom studio at Wyncolls Road where customers can select from the leading

Above: *The warehouse in the 1970s.*
Right: *Handling traditional heating materials.*

Southend-on-Sea, besides the two Colchester branches. Up in Suffolk there are branches in Ipswich, Bury St Edmunds, Stowmarket and Sudbury. Essex Heating also operates from two branches in Norfolk at Norwich and Kings Lynn, while across in Cambridgeshire branches are situated in Peterborough and Cambridge. Hertfordshire and London are serviced by the Watford branch. The business has plans to expand further into London, Kent and East Anglia in the not too distant future. As well as the Essex Heating branches the company also trades under the name PHS (Plumbing & Heating Supplies) in the county of Kent in Chatham and Tunbridge Wells.

The excellent and widespread reputation which Essex Heating Supplies Ltd enjoys today is due in no small part to the commitment of the firm's experienced and professional staff, who are always willing to learn and ready to pass on their customers the information which they have gained. The company recognises that there is no substitute for a well-trained, knowledgeable and efficient workforce which customers enjoy dealing with, and is very selective in recruiting new employees. Each branch aims to provide a personal service to its customers, and in this way the company is able to provide comprehensive modern facilities and high levels of customer support which match those of the national merchants, without sacrificing the 'local feel' which many clients prefer.

Essex Heating Supplies Ltd's lively and refreshing approach has overcome the economic challenges of the past decades to build up an enviable reputation, a loyal client base, an impressive network of branches and a comprehensive stock - and all this has been achieved in just 30 years. We look forward to reporting on even greater achievements by this dynamic young Colchester-born company in the year 2030.

Above: *Part of today's fleet.* ***Top:*** *The distribution centre at Severalls Industrial Park from the air.*

Carrying the load

The Haulage business B T Cullum and Son, now operating from its premises in Tiptree, began its life nearly 80 years ago in 1922.

At just 17 years of age the young Bertie Thomas Cullum, who was known to all as Tom, founded the loyal family business that was to become B T Cullum and Son. Tom used the new T Type Ford Lorry, which his father had bought for £70, to carry and deliver milk, wood and agricultural products from Salcot where they were then based, to local villages. This work was a welcome break from his other thatching, hay cutting and straw binding jobs and was to become the full time haulage business that it is today.

The advent of the war years brought with them a temporary change of direction for the company. During this time the Cullum lorries were put to use as transport for the Home Guard.

After the end of the war years the company resumed business as usual. Years later in 1954, Tom's son Anthony, or Tony as he is known, joined the business earning it the name B T Cullum and Son and securing its reputation as a family business. At that time, Tom and Tony's main contracts were for agricultural transportation of straw and hay. However, they also branched out into the transportation of flowers, plants, shrubs, fruit and vegetables from local nurseries to famous London markets such as Spitalfields and Covent Garden.

In 1972, some 50 years after the business was established, the transportation of goods to the London markets was halted and instead, the whole business concentrated on general haulage in which it still specialises today.

Nowadays, Tony takes care of the everyday running of the business. B T Cullum and Son now employ a team of drivers who are all local to the area. The 40 tonne tractor units in operation today carry loads throughout the UK and when contracts dictate, to Europe. Although the business has expanded throughout the years and now mainly conducts contract haulage, B T Cullum and Son have sustained their reputation as a personal, faithful family business still firmly rooted in the local area.

Above left: *Tom Cullum in 1968.*
Below and bottom: *Part of the fleet in 1958.*

Queen Street in a picture dating from the late 1930s

Acknowledgments

The publishers would like to thank the following people and organisations for their help in the production of this book

Colchester Museums
who supplied the images found on pages 1, 3 - 39, 48 - 76 & 104

Richard Shackle, Local Studies Library, Colchester Library

Thanks are also due to
Andrew Mitchell who penned the editorial text and
Ann Ramsdale for her copywriting skills